KnOCK 'em DEaD

SOCIAL NETWORKING

SOCIAL NETWORKING

For Job Search and Professional Success

MARTIN YATE, CPC

New York Times bestselling author

AVON, MASSACHUSETTS

Published by
Adams Media, a division of F+W Media, Inc.
57 Littlefield Street, Avon, MA 02322. U.S.A.
www.adamsmedia.com

ISBN 10: 1-4405-6971-1
ISBN 13: 978-1-4405-6971-5
eISBN 10: 1-4405-7439-1
eISBN 13: 978-1-4405-7439-9

Printed in the United States of America.

10   9   8   7   6   5   4   3   2   1

Cover design by Sylvia McArdle.
Photo by Lori Ambler.

This book is available at quantity discounts for bulk purchases.
For information, please call 1-800-289-0963.

CONTENTS

Social Networking: The Key to a Successful Future

Your Whirlwind Life

Like it or not, technology is triggering irreversible changes in the way you and I live our lives, and in every aspect of the way we work. There is nothing we can do to stop the torrent of innovation that technology makes possible, so the choice facing us all is simple: Adapt and flourish, leveraging the vast potential of social networking to find financial security, professional fulfillment, and personal happiness, or get left behind.

Financial Security

Technological innovations, especially the meteoric growth of social networking, have changed the way companies recruit and hire, and this means that you need to adapt your job search and career management strategies for your career to remain buoyant. Almost overnight, a strong social media presence has become a must-have for every working professional, but this isn't necessarily bad news, because social networking can give you greater control over the direction of all aspects of your life.

From a professional perspective, you need a presence on at least a few social media platforms (networking sites), because recruiters use them as a major new recruitment resource. The social media platforms you choose will all need to reflect the same messaging about who you are as a professional, while at the same time, you will need to build and use them in ways that make you discoverable by recruiters and your professional peers. Adapting to these changes is so important to your well-being that if you don't, you will gradually become professionally invisible and your financial stability will suffer as a result.

Fulfillment

While social networking has revolutionized the way you approach a job search, it has equal potential to revolutionize the way you manage your career, empowering you with new tools for achieving success, fulfillment, and happiness.

Beyond managing your existing professional career, social networking allows you to connect with the people who share your passions and dreams. Even better, technology has delivered powerful new tools for turning your dreams into income streams.

For instance, when I built the first *Knock 'em Dead* website, I envisaged having my own TV station and broadcasting career-saving advice to the world. However, while the technology existed, the costs were prohibitive. Twelve years later, the folks at Google+, one of the major professional networking sites, made very similar capabilities available to us all; you, me, anyone can start a global TV broadcasting system tomorrow and do it for little or nothing. If even global broadcasting is now a reality for anyone who wants to do it, imagine what else might be possible: Whatever your goals and dreams, there are almost certainly new tools available to help you achieve them and, in the process, bring new meaning to your life.

Happiness

Social networking is even changing who we meet, pursue common interests with, date, and marry. The ads for dating sites like Match.com say you are three times more likely to date and marry using an online system. This new way of meeting people through social networking is now completely accepted, because it has empowered us to meet people we would never have met before and then forge meaningful relationships with them. I met my wife Angela this way, and although we lived in the same city, there is no question that without social networking our paths would never have crossed.

Social Networking and Your Career

Social networking has become an essential new tool for achieving your professional goals—and for maintaining success over the arc of a long career. No matter what your age or professional status, the only three constants in twenty-first-century professional life are:

1. **There is no job security**—"Work hard and be loyal" is corporate Kool-Aid, which will flow freely until they choose to dump your sorry ass in a restructuring, automate your job out of existence, or export it to a country where someone will do the same work for less money. You cannot rely on employers anymore; you need to take more responsibility for guiding the path of your career. The power of social networking can help.

2. **The digital era is here to stay**, and it has brought about a revolution in how we do everything at work and at play. This sudden change can be a little overwhelming if you didn't grow up in the digital world, but this is also a time

of enormous opportunity, and it offers you the tools to develop your capabilities and redefine your professional self, in the process gaining more control of your career.

3. **Change is constant** in modern professional life. With job security largely a thing of the past, you must learn to anticipate and manage change, rather than being sideswiped by it. The people you meet through intelligently built social networks share many of your concerns, and so they are far more motivated to help you navigate the ups and downs of a long work life than corporations, which have little concern for how your life plays out.

Social networking is your new launch pad for a more businesslike approach to managing the path of your career for the future. Making a success of your life is a long-term and complex challenge, and connectivity with others who are motivated to help you is a critical component. In the following pages, I'll show you how to build these social networks and use them in job search and career management.

PART I

Your Social Networking Brand

CHAPTER 1

HOW TO LIVE LIFE ON YOUR TERMS

. . . And Get What You Want Out of Life

Mastering social networking isn't brain surgery—it is a professional skill that, once integrated into your life, will help you navigate the twists and turns of a long career and enrich your life in other ways.

In this book, we'll talk about the social networking skills that will help you execute a successful job search with the help of robust professional networks and develop new career management strategies. There's a commonsense logic behind every social networking tactic you'll learn, and they'll all mesh seamlessly together into a practical strategy for managing the progress of your career. You can get a social network–integrated job search started within a week, and reap the rewards for the rest of your career.

Focused Social Messaging

The first lesson we learn in the professional world is: "Your customers are always right," and the second lesson is: "Find out what your customers want and then sell it to them." The same goes for social networking. It is important that the messaging of your social media profiles and social networking activities reflect a brand that employers find compelling. Your social networking activities can make a significant contribution to your success in life, but first you need to appreciate corporate priorities, and then brand yourself as the kind of professional who understands and supports them.

The corporation is a complex piece of moneymaking machinery that delivers products and services for its customers in exchange for income. In turn, every job is a small but important cog in this complex moneymaking machine. If the company can redesign its machinery to do without a particular cog (automation) or can find a cheaper/younger cog or outsource your job to Mumbai, it's going to do so.

Most professional jobs, like yours, exist because the company hasn't yet been able to simplify them enough for export to a country with cheaper labor costs or automate them out of existence altogether. This is because, in your professional area, problems arise that require both technical expertise and judgment to solve. Consequently, employers first look for someone who has the *technical skills* to execute the deliverables of the job, and then the supporting *transferable skills* that empower a candidate to solve the problems that typically occur within that particular area of expertise. On top of this, the employer hopes to hire someone who understands the professional territory the job covers well enough to *anticipate and prevent* many of these problems from arising in the first place, and to *solve* them efficiently when they do arise.

No matter what your job title, essentially you are always hired to be a problem solver within a specific area of expertise. Think about the nuts and bolts of any job you've held. At its heart, that job is chiefly concerned with the *anticipation, prevention, and solution of problems.* Over the coming pages, this fundamental insight will help you develop a resilient social networking brand that resonates with employers' needs and implement the social networking tactics and strategies that will help you establish your credentials and get more interviews and better job offers.

Take Control of Your Career

Your parents were born into a world in which hard work, dedication, and sacrifice led to long-term job security and a steady, predictable climb up the ladder of success. But for you and your peers—as well as for those of your elders still employed—the world has changed. Companies still expect hard work, dedication, and sacrifice, but you are expendable.

If you are ready to become the architect of your own success, this new digitally dominated world is a place of enormous opportunity. But if you *aren't* prepared to take responsibility for the success of your professional life, a first job turns into another identical one a year or two down the road, and then another, and after seven to ten years all you'll see are the backs of people who were your peers at the start of your career. Then in your forties, you will realize your so-called "career" has just been an ongoing series of very similar jobs that are taking you nowhere, and by fifty, when wage and age discrimination begin to kick in, you'll be lost and depressed because somehow it all passed you by. Where such people go wrong is in not being prepared to develop the career management and networking skills that give them control over the quality and outcomes of their lives.

Enlightened Self-Interest and Social Networking

Social networking is only important to the degree to which it serves your needs, so we have to put it in the context of a central idea in career management strategy. You have one life to live, so don't waste it on blind loyalty to companies that do not care what becomes of you; instead, adopt a commitment to *enlightened self-interest*: putting *your* survival and happiness first. This means placing your financial security and personal fulfillment front and center in your life. Stop thinking of yourself as a "company man" or some poor sap looking for a job, and start to think of yourself as a company, a financial entity that needs to maintain a steady cash flow for (if you are at the start of your career) fifty years or more. The first step in taking control of your professional destiny, your life, and your economic well-being is exercising the same forethought, objectivity, and self-interest as a corporation.

Start thinking of yourself as a company—as MeInc.

As MeInc, you have products and services to sell to your customers (employers). These are the professional skills and experience you accumulate as you work. *These products and services have to fulfill the needs of your customers, or the sale will go to a competitor.* To remain competitive over the course of your career, it will help to structure the activities of MeInc along the same lines as successful corporations; you'll need:

- *Research & Development (R&D):* To identify and develop emerging skills with the maximum marketplace appeal. You have to monitor evolving market demands on an ongoing basis to develop the skills that employers need. This will help you establish a social media presence (or brand) that keeps current with marketplace demands.

- *Marketing and Public Relations:* The social networks you build are your most powerful tools for establishing professional credibility and ensuring that MeInc becomes visible as a desirable brand to an ever-widening circle, expanding outwards through your department, the company, your local professional community, and beyond, as your career plans dictate.
- *Strategic Planning:* To monitor the general health of your profession and your employer in particular. This enables you to plan and time the strategic job changes that take you to new employers, and to change careers—*on your timetable.* Working with R&D and Marketing, your Strategic Planning activities will complement the social networking activities that help you monitor professional opportunities and strategies for researching the pursuit of completely new revenue streams.
- *Finance:* Live up to your dreams, not your income. You live in a world dominated by 24/7 advertising media, and your exposure encourages you to fritter away your income on the instant gratification drummed into your head by advertising. To control your destiny and make your dreams come true, you have to break free of this indoctrination and invest yourself, your time, and your income in the activities that will make MeInc successful and give you the opportunity for a fulfilling life.
- *Sales:* The varied *communication skills* that enable you to put together a resume that works, generate job interviews, and turn those interviews into job offers. Beyond this, Sales includes tactics for gaining job security, winning promotions, and using your social networking skills to execute job searches and career changes on your own timetable.

Social Networking and a
Financially Secure and Fulfilled Life

To succeed in life, you have to take responsibility for achieving your goals and guiding the development of your career. Social networking is one of the most effective and flexible tools you have at your disposal to make this happen. In a job market revolutionized by technological change, integrating a social media presence and effective social networking strategies into your career management plans will dramatically improve your chances of living the life you want to live. In the next chapter, we'll get started by talking about the skills that form the basis of your social media brand.

CHAPTER 2

THE FOUNDATIONS OF CAREER SUCCESS

There are certain words you see in almost every job posting: *communication skills, multitasking, teamwork, creativity, critical thinking, leadership, determination, productivity, motivation*, and a few more we'll discuss shortly. These words represent a secret language of success that few job hunters ever show that they understand. The ones who do "get it" are also the ones who get the interviews, job offers, and subsequent raises and promotions.

The words and phrases of this secret language represent the foundation of all enduring professional success, because whatever your job may be, they embody the skills that enable you to do that job well. They are known as *transferable skills and professional values* because no matter what the job, the profession, or the elevation of that job, these skills and values make the difference between success and failure. They are the skills that all employers look for and that you should embody in the *professional brand* reflected in your social media presence.

The Professional Everyone Wants to Work With

Over the years, I've read a lot of books about finding jobs, winning promotions, and managing your career. One theme that runs through many of them is just plain dumb: the advice to "just be yourself." Let me explain why this thinking is wrongheaded. Remember that first day on your first job, when you went to find the coffee machine? You found it, and there, stuck on the wall was a handwritten sign reading:

> YOUR MOTHER DOESN'T WORK HERE
> PICK UP AFTER YOURSELF

You thought, "Pick up after myself? Gee, guess I've got to develop a new way of doing things." And so you started to observe and emulate the more successful professionals around you. You developed new skills and ways of conducting yourself, in effect creating a separate *professional self* that enabled you to survive in the professional world.

How well you develop these skills and integrate them into your daily behavior and social messaging will have considerable impact on the degree of your professional success.

These are the skills and values that employers all over the world in every industry and profession are anxious to find in candidates from the entry level to the boardroom. They are the foundation of every successful career.

Transferable Skills and Professional Values

These skills are the foundation of all the professional success you will experience in this or any other career you may pursue over the course of your life, because they underlie your ability to execute the responsibilities of your job effectively, whatever that job may be. These are the *transferable skills and professional values* that recruiters and hiring managers look for in potential candidates; they get you hired and help you make a success of the new opportunity.

You should reflect your particular mix of *transferable skills and professional values* in your resume and social media profiles and embody them in the way you execute your responsibilities and interact with others. Do this and you will attract networking contacts of similarly high caliber. These skills and values will speed the conclusion of a job search, help you get off on the right foot in a new job, and make that job more secure by earning you access to the inner circle that exists within every department . . . where all the plum assignments, raises, and promotions live. You'll find that you already have some of these skills and values to a greater or lesser degree, and if you are committed to making a success of your life, you'll continue to develop all of them further.

Transferable Skills	Professional Values
Technical	*Motivation and Energy*
Critical Thinking	*Commitment and Reliability*
Communication	*Determination*
Multitasking	*Pride and Integrity*
Creativity	*Productivity*
Teamwork	*Systems and Procedures*
Leadership	

As you read about each *transferable skill and professional value* you may, for example, read about *communication*, and think, "Yes, I can see how *communication skills* are important in all jobs and at all levels of the promotional ladder, and, hallelujah, I have good *communication skills.*" When this happens, take the time to recall examples of the role each different *communication skill* (there are eight of them) plays in each of your work responsibilities. This will help you create the right tone in your social media profile narratives.

You will also find that there are skills you need to work on. Whenever you identify a *transferable skill* that needs work, you have found a *professional development project*: improving that skill. Such *professional development projects* show that you are truly engaged with the things that make the difference between successful professionals and the rest.

Your skill development activities can also become part of your social networking. For example, if you were working on *multitasking skills* (time management and organization), you could post on your social media profile updates: "Just read a great piece on time management and organization . . ." and then add a link. This shows recruiters that you are involved in developing important skills and also positions you as a source of useful information for your networking contacts, which can only add to your credibility and the creation of a desirable brand. Your work in developing these skills will repay you for the rest of your working life, no matter how you make a living today or in the future.

Transferable Skills
TECHNICAL SKILLS

The *technical skills* of your job are the foundation of success within your current profession; without them you won't even land a job, much less keep it for long or win a promotion. They speak to your *ability* to do the job: those essential skills necessary for the day-to-day execution of your duties. These *technical skills* vary from profession to profession and do not refer to anything technical *as such* or to technology.

Some of the most in-demand *technical skills* across a wide range of professions include:

- Social Networking skills
- Selling skills
- Project Management skills
- Six Sigma skills
- Lean Management skills
- Quantitative Analysis skills
- Theory Development and Conceptual Thinking skills
- Counseling and Mentoring skills
- Customer Resource Management (CRM) skills
- Research skills

Technology Skills

It is a given that one of the *technical skills* essential to every job is technological competence. You must be proficient in all the technology and Internet-based applications relevant to your work. Even when you are not working in a technology field, strong *technology skills* (as they apply to your work) will enhance your stability and help you leverage professional growth. It is pretty much a given that you need to be computer literate to hold down any job today, as just about every job expects competency with Microsoft Word and e-mail. Similarly, Excel and Power-Point are becoming essential. I can't think of any professional jobs where you wouldn't be called on to have minimal familiarity with them.

Any employer is going to welcome a staff member who knows her way around spreadsheets and databases, can update a web-page, or is knowledgeable in CRM.

Some of the *technology skills* that enhance employability on nontechnological jobs include:

- Database management skills
- Spreadsheet skills
- Online and offline document layout skills

- Presentation media skills
- Other communication media skills

Eventually more and more of these skills will become specific requirements of the jobs of the future, but until then, possession of these skills will add a special sauce to your candidacy for any job.

Staying current with the essential *technical* and *technology skills* of your chosen career path is the keystone of your professional stability and growth. *Technical skills,* while transferable, vary from profession to profession, so some of your current *technical skills* will only be transferable within your current profession.

CRITICAL THINKING SKILLS

As we noted earlier, your job, whatever it is, exists to prevent problems from arising within your area of expertise, and to solve those problems efficiently when they do. *Critical thinking,* also referred to as *analytical* or *problem-solving skills*, represents a systematic approach to dealing with the challenges presented by your work. *Critical thinking skills* enable you to think through a problem, define the challenge and its possible solutions, and then evaluate and implement the best solution from all available options. Fifty percent of the success of any project is in the preparation, and *critical thinking* is at the heart of that preparation.

COMMUNICATION SKILLS

Every professional job today demands good *communication skills*, but what are they?

When the professional world talks about *communication skills*, it isn't just referring to verbal communication, but to four primary skills and four supportive skills. The primary *communication skills* are:

- Verbal skills—what you say and how you say it.
- Listening skills—*listening* to understand, rather than just waiting your turn to talk.
- Writing skills—clear written *communication* creates a lasting impression of who you are and is essential for success in any professional career.
- Technological communication skills—your ability to evaluate the suitability of alternative *communication* media and then choose the medium most appropriate to your message and audience.

The four supportive *communication skills* are:

- Grooming and dress—your appearance tells others who you are and how you feel about yourself, and establishes a level of respect before you ever say a word.
- Social graces—how you behave toward others in all situations, which defines your professionalism.
- Body language—this displays how you're feeling deep inside, a form of communication that predates speech. For truly effective *communication*, what your mouth says must be in harmony with what your body says.
- Emotional IQ—your emotional self-awareness and consequently your maturity in dealing with others in unfamiliar or stressful situations.

All the component skills of good *communication* are interconnected—for example, good *verbal skills* require both *listening* and *writing skills*. Likewise, they are all connected with the other *transferable skills and professional values*; for example, effective *communication* requires *critical thinking skills* to accurately process incoming information and enable you to present your outgoing communications persuasively in light of the interests and sophistication of your audience.

When you develop competence in the eight components of good *communication skills*, you'll gain enormous control over what you can achieve and how you are treated. Few people with well-rounded *communication skills* fail in life.

MULTITASKING

This is one of the most desirable skills of the new era. According to numerous studies, however, the *multitasking* demands of modern professional life are causing massive frustration and meltdowns for professionals everywhere. This is a misconception.

The problem is *not multitasking*, rather it is the erroneous assumption that *multitasking* means being reactive to *all* incoming stimuli and therefore jumping around from one task to another as the emergency of the moment dictates. Such a definition of *multitasking* would of course leave you feeling that wild horses are attached to your extremities and tearing you limb from limb.

MULTITASKING BUILDING BLOCKS

Instead, *multitasking* abilities are built on sound *time management and organizational skills*. They're based on three building blocks:

1. Getting organized and staying that way
2. Establishing priorities every day
3. Managing your time effectively

These three building blocks are more easily achieved than you'd imagine with the Plan, Do, Review Cycle.

THE PLAN, DO, REVIEW CYCLE

At the end of every day, review what you've accomplished:

- What happened: A.M. and P.M.?
- What went well? Do more of it.
- What went wrong? How do I fix it?
- What projects do I need to move forward tomorrow?
- List all tomorrow's activities and rank the importance of each one.
  A—Must be completed by end of day
  B—Good to be completed by end of day
  C—To be completed if there is spare time from A and B priorities
- Make a prioritized To Do list, with every activity rated A, B, or C.
- Stick to the prioritized list.

Doing this at the end of the day keeps you informed about what you have achieved, and lets you know that you have invested your time in the most important activities today and will tomorrow, so you feel better, sleep better, and come in tomorrow focused and ready to rock.

CREATIVITY

Someone is seen as creative when his ideas produce tangible results. There's a big difference between *creativity* and just having ideas. Ideas are like headaches: We all get them once in a while, and like headaches, they disappear as mysteriously as they arrived. *Creativity,* on the other hand, is the ability to develop those ideas with the skills that bring them to life.

Creativity, in its professional context, grows from a thorough understanding of your job and all the factors that impact the successful outcomes of your activities. This enables you to see the *patterns* that lie behind challenges, and so come up with solutions that others might have missed because they were mired in details and didn't have the "big picture" frame of reference that enabled you to step back and view the issue in its larger context.

Creativity is empowered by:

- Your *critical thinking skills*, applied within an area of *technical expertise* (that area of expertise where your *technical skills* give you a frame of reference for what works and what doesn't).
- Your *multitasking skills*, which in combination with your *critical thinking* and *technical skills* allow you to break your challenge down into specific steps and determine which approach is best.
- Your *communication skills*, which allow you to explain your approach persuasively to your target audience.
- Your *teamwork* and *leadership skills*, which enable you to enlist others and bring the idea to fruition.

Teamwork

Companies depend on teams because the professional world revolves around the complex challenges of making money, and such complexities require teams of people to provide ongoing solutions. This means that you must work efficiently and respectfully with other people who have totally different responsibilities, backgrounds, objectives, and areas of expertise. It's true that individual initiative is important, but as a professional, much of the really important work you do will be done as a member of a group. Your long-term success requires that you learn the arts of cooperation, team-based decision making, and team *communication*.

Teamwork demands that a commitment to the team and its success always comes first. This means you take on a task because it needs to be done, not because it makes you look good.

As a *team player* you:

- Always cooperate.
- Always make decisions based on team goals.
- Always work for the common good.
- Always keep colleagues informed.
- Always keep commitments.
- Always share credit, never blame.

If you become a successful leader in your professional life, it's a given that you were first a reliable *team player*, because a leader must understand the dynamics of *teamwork* before she can lead a team. When *teamwork* is coupled with the other *transferable skills and professional values*, the result is greater responsibility, raises, and promotions.

LEADERSHIP SKILLS

Leadership is the most complex of all the *transferable skills*. Notice how you are willing to follow true leaders but don't fall in line with people who don't respect you and who don't have your best interests at heart. As a leader, when others believe in your competence, and believe you have everyone's success as your goal, they will follow you.

Leadership is a critical skill for long-term survival as a manager, and just as critical if you want to break into the ranks of management:

- Your job as a leader is to help your team succeed, and your *teamwork skills* give you the knowledge to understand what will pull a team together.
- Your *technical* expertise, *critical thinking*, and *creativity skills* help you correctly define the challenges your team faces and give you the wisdom to guide them toward solutions.

- There's nothing more demoralizing than a leader who can't clearly articulate why you're doing what you're doing, so your *communication skills* encourage team members to *buy into* your directives and goals.
- Your *creativity* comes from the wide frame of reference you have for your job and the profession and industry in which you work, enabling you to come up with solutions that others might not have seen.
- Your *multitasking skills*, based on sound *time management and organizational abilities*, enable you to create a time-sensitive blueprint for success and your team to take ownership of the task and deliver the expected results on time.

When your actions inspire others to think more, learn more, do more, and become more, you are becoming a leader. This will ultimately be recognized and rewarded with promotion into and up the ranks of management. *Leadership* is a combination and outgrowth of all the *transferable skills* plus the clear presence of all the *professional values* we are about to discuss. Leaders aren't born; they are self-made by professionals who invest themselves in their future success.

Professional Values

Professional values are a set of core beliefs that enable professionals to determine the right judgment call in any given situation. Highly prized by employers, this value system is integral to, and supportive of, each of the *transferable skills*.

MOTIVATION AND ENERGY

You always give that extra effort to get the job done and get it done right. *Motivation and energy* express themselves in your engagement with and enthusiasm for your work and profession. They involve an eagerness to learn and grow professionally, and a willingness to take the rough with the smooth in pursuit of meaningful goals. *Motivation* is invariably expressed by the *energy* you demonstrate in your work.

COMMITMENT AND RELIABILITY

The *committed* professional is willing to do whatever it takes to get a job done, whenever and for however long it takes to get the job done, even if that includes duties that might not appear in a job description and that might be perceived by less enlightened colleagues as beneath them. This means dedication to your profession, and the empowerment that comes from knowing how your part contributes to the whole. Your *commitment* expresses itself in your *reliability*.

DETERMINATION

The *determination* you display in tackling the problems your work dumps on your desk every day speaks of a professional who does not back off when the going gets tough.

The *determined* professional has decided to make a difference with her presence every day, because it is the *right* thing to do, and because it makes the time go faster.

She is willing to do whatever it takes to get a job done, and she will demonstrate that *determination* on behalf of colleagues who share the same values. It's a *professional value* that marks you as someone who always chooses to be part of the solution.

PRIDE AND INTEGRITY

If a job's worth doing, it's worth doing right. *Pride* in your work means attention to detail and a *commitment* to doing your very best. *Integrity* applies to all your dealings, whether with coworkers, management, customers, or vendors. Honesty really *is* the best policy.

PRODUCTIVITY

The successful professional always works toward *productivity* in his areas of responsibility through efficiencies of time, resources, money, and effort.

ECONOMY

Remember the word "frugal"? It doesn't mean miserliness. It means making the most of what you've got, using everything with the greatest efficiency. Companies that know how to be frugal with their resources will prosper in good times and bad, and if you know how to be frugal, you'll do the same.

SYSTEMS AND PROCEDURES

This is a natural outgrowth of all the other *transferable skills and professional values*. Your *commitment* to your profession gives you an appreciation of the need for the *systems and procedures* that help a company function effectively. Consequently, you understand and always follow the chain of command.

If ways of doing things don't make sense or are interfering with efficiency and profitability, you work through the system to get them changed. You don't implement your own "improved" procedures or encourage others to do so.

Transferable Skills and Your Social Media Brand

When you are seen to embody these *transferable skills and professional values* in your work and in the ways you interact with the people of your professional world, you will become known and respected by your coworkers and management as a thorough professional. When you further embody these *transferable skills and professional values* in your social networking activities, you can begin to differentiate your candidacy in a job search, and dramatically improve the growth and quality of your networks.

The effectiveness of your social media presence rests on the image, or brand, you create for your social media profiles, and on how that brand is expressed in your networking activities. We'll look at brand building next.

CHAPTER 3

A Professional Brand for a Lifetime of Networking

Your *professional brand* is the face you show to the world of work. If you haven't thought about your professional identity before, now is the time to start, because when you create a social media profile (and a resume) you are defining how the world sees you. The result is called a brand. If the promises made by your *brand* are professionally desirable and are substantiated by the tone, narrative, and examples seen in your social media profiles, you'll become more visible to recruiters, receive more and better interviews and job offers, and your reputation will grow.

Brand Versus Reputation

Your *brand* is how you capture and promote all that is best and unique about the professional you. The essential marketing tools that define your brand are your resume(s) and social media profiles. Your professional *reputation* is the way other professionals see you, based on what they have read about you and more importantly what personal interaction tells them about you. Together, your brand and reputation should complement each other, but creating a brand and building a professional reputation takes time.

For one thing, it's much easier to brand products and companies than it is to brand people because:

- Companies have teams of people to work on product branding, which, while a particular product may change a little every year, will remain essentially constant in nature and function.
- People, on the other hand, are in a constant state of change; they change jobs and careers with such predictable regularity that a professional's brand has to be flexible—has to be able to evolve without losing its identity.

Branding is the process of drawing attention to what makes your product special: those attributes that mark you as more desirable than other products on the market. Once you do this, you can formally capture them in your social media profiles and resume. Defining the persona that you want to show to your professional world, and then keeping that message consistent and visible in your social media profiles, resume, and all you say, do, and write (your social media posts and tweets, etc.) to support this messaging is what constitutes a *professional brand*.

So your *professional brand* is a thoughtful way of shaping how you are seen in your professional world. When you create a *professional brand* as part of an overall career management strategy, it gives *you* focus and *motivation*, and over time offers *others* an easy way to differentiate you from your competition.

You Must Have a Relevant and Truthful Brand

Professional branding also creates challenges because whatever you say in social media profiles and resumes will be examined, and if your word is seen to be exaggeration, hyperbole, or outright fabrication, it *will destroy* the integrity of your brand and all that you are trying to achieve with it. People get around: Large professions become small communities as the years roll by, so you must be respectful of the collective memory of your professional community as you create your brand, in order to protect whatever reputation you have nurtured up to this point in your career and as you move forward.

Your brand should reflect the professional skills, behaviors, and values that your customers consider desirable. You could, of course, build a brand out of your wacky personality and interests—as I have seen suggested—but a thinking professional will immediately recognize that personality and hobbies are way down the list of priorities for recruiters and hiring managers, who are looking for:

- Technical competency
- The *transferable skills* that encourage successful execution of the job's deliverables
- The problem-solving capabilities for the problems that the work throws up every day
- Someone who can fit into a team and work well with others
- Reliability and complementary *professional values*

Once you define the attributes that will appeal to your target employers, the narrative of your social media profiles and your resume needs to strike the right balance: If you underpromise, you lose recruiters' attention. If you overpromise, the employer might initially be attracted, but when you are revealed as all thunder and no lightning during your job interviews, the deception will backfire. You have to be able to deliver on the promises made by your brand; it's a process that takes time and effort, but a powerful and conscientiously maintained brand has networking benefits that can positively impact your career for years to come.

The Geico Gecko Didn't Happen Overnight

Your brand is what makes you memorable. All the most outstanding commercial brands have a distinct personality; that green gecko with the funny English accent immediately springs to mind.

The question is, what came first, Geico or the gecko? The product came first; the insurance giant was successful way before the gecko was created. As a company, Geico worked hard for seventy years to build a reputation, and only recently invested in branding. The personality of an established commercial brand can be created quickly: That quirky gecko was created and launched inside of twelve months. But the engaging public face of Geico only came to us from the blood, sweat, and tears of (at least) two large, highly creative teams of advertising pros, and at the cost of many millions of dollars. The point is partly that branding takes time and effort, and just as importantly for you, that branding has to be based on solid and professional work behavior: You can't build a great brand if you don't do a great job at work.

Branding is the process of creating a distinctive and memorable image of your *professional persona* and, over time, imprinting that *professional persona* onto the collective memory of your professional community (your customer base).

What Customers (Your Employers) Want and Need

A well-conceived brand can give momentum to a product, but remember that *a great product comes before the packaging*. To be successful, the public face you create in developing your *professional brand* must be based on a firm foundation of the skills, behaviors, and values desirable to your customers.

It all comes down to this: If you want a brand that helps you succeed professionally, you must consider what your customers want (they don't want a lizard with a funny accent), and then develop a brand that *resonates with the priorities of those customers.*

Because brand development takes time, your priority for this year and this job search is to build the core of your brand: Strive to integrate the *technical* and *transferable skills and professional values* that are foundational to all professional success, because these are what your customers want most, want now, and will always want—they are the basis of a durable *professional brand.* Build a solid core for your brand, own these skills and values in everything you do, and use them to help brand yourself as a well-rounded professional in your social media profiles, networking activities, resume, and any other marketing materials and activities.

When your brand supports a product (you) built to meet the needs of the customer, it will make a real contribution to your credibility, visibility, and ultimately your long-term success, because thriving professionals recognize in others what it takes, and this recognition results in a natural attraction.

Selling to Your Customers' Needs

Start with the first rule of advertising, marketing, public relations, and sales: *Sell to the customers' needs.* Look through their eyes and see the world as they do, and you'll see what they value. Take a moment to write down the messages you have absorbed so far about what your customers value. Your list will read something like this:

My customers demand:

- Technical competency in the skills of my profession (*Technical Skills*)
- Competency with the technology applications of the profession (*Technology Skills*)
- *Motivation and Energy, Commitment and Reliability, Determination, Pride and Integrity, Productivity,* and adherence to *Systems and Procedures*
- Familiarity with the nuances of the profession and industry
- Results-driven, goal- rather than task-oriented people (*Critical Thinking, Multitasking, Determination*)
- *Multitasking skills* based on sound time management and organization
- Conscientious work habits that prevent problems from arising and solve them when they do (*Critical Thinking and Creativity*)

Now and throughout your career, your brand should position you as someone who's current, competent, committed, easy and pleasant to work with, and a thorough professional. Taking the above points and making them the core of your *professional brand* will mark you as someone worth getting to know—and that is one of the most important goals of your branding efforts.

Your Brand and First Impressions

When your branding efforts result in approaches by recruiters, your brand as it is expressed in written materials has to withstand the light of screening interviews and then face-to-face meetings. The impression you leave during these initial contacts is affected by the following considerations:

- What your appearance says about your success, sophistication, professional awareness, and sense of self.
- What your social graces—the way you conduct yourself, say about your professionalism. You'll be evaluated by the way you conduct yourself during telephone screenings and when you meet in person; you'll never reach the corner office by being rude to people and using your knife and fork like hunting weapons.
- Your body language
- Your emotional maturity

Emphasize all the *transferable skills* you develop with the four supporting *communication skills*—dress, social graces, body language, and emotional maturity—and the *verbal* and *written communication skills* that influence all professional interactions, and you will have a set of behaviors that will be admired by all employers. These will serve as the basis for a solid reputation and a brand that is flexible and that will grow over time, no matter what paths you pursue in your professional life.

How to Identify Your Competitive Difference

Your ability to first identify and then develop the universal *transferable skills and professional values* as the foundations for your brand is a good start, but it isn't enough. It's time to think about how your activities at work demonstrate your unique way of embodying these skills and values.

The following Competitive Difference Questionnaire (CDQ) will help you identify the skill and behavior differentiators that make you unique and that, once discovered, will become components of your *professional brand*. It will then be natural to integrate them into your social media profiles and resume. You can find a link to a downloadable version of this questionnaire on the Downloads page at *www.knockemdead.com*.

The Competitive Difference Questionnaire (CDQ)

What are the four key deliverables of your job?

1. _____
2. _____
3. _____
4. _____

Identify the *technical skills* of your job that you see as particular strengths.

1. _____
2. _____
3. _____

Identify the *technical skills* that you should mark for further professional development.

1. _____
2. _____
3. _____

How are you going to go about developing them?

_____

_____

Identify the *technology skills* that you see as particular strengths.

1. _____
2. _____
3. _____

Which of the *transferable skills and professional values* have you marked for further professional development? What are you going to do?

1. _____

2. _____

3. _____

List and prioritize the *transferable skills and professional values* that best capture the essence of the *professional you*: *Communication, Commitment and Reliability, Pride and Integrity, Productivity and Economy, Critical Thinking, Creativity, Teamwork, Multitasking, Leadership, Determination,* and *Systems and Procedures.*

1. _____

2. _____

3. _____

4. _____

5. _____

6. _____

7. _____

8. _____

9. _____

10. _____

What *transferable skills and professional values* or other characteristics do you share with top performers in your department/profession?

1. _____

2. _____

3. _____

What have you achieved with these qualities?

_____

_____

_____

What makes you different from others with whom you have worked?

_____

_____

_____

What do you see as your four most defining *transferable skills and professional values*, and how does each help your performance?

1. _____
2. _____
3. _____
4. _____

How do your most defining professional traits help you contribute to the department's success?

1. _____
2. _____
3. _____
4. _____

Why do you stand out in your job/department/profession?

_____

_____

_____

If you don't stand out and you want to, define how the people you admire stand out. What plans do you have for change?

_____

_____

_____

In what ways are you better than others who hold the same title?

_____

_____

What excites you most about your professional responsibilities?

_____

_____

What are your biggest achievements in these areas?

_____

_____

What do your peers say about you?

_____

_____

What does management say about you?

_____

_____

What do your reports say about you?

_____

_____

_____

What are your top four professional skills?
Skill #1: _____
Quantifiable achievements with this skill:

_____

_____

_____

Skill #2: _____
Quantifiable achievements with this skill:

_____

_____

_____

Skill #3: _____
Quantifiable achievements with this skill:

_____

_____

_____

Skill #4: _____
Quantifiable achievements with this skill:

_____

_____

_____

What are your top four *leadership* skills?
Skill #1: _____
Quantifiable achievements with this skill:

_____

_____

_____

Skill #2: _____

Quantifiable achievements with this skill:

_____

_____

_____

Skill #3: _____

Quantifiable achievements with this skill:

_____

_____

_____

Skill #4: _____

Quantifiable achievements with this skill:

_____

_____

_____

What gives you greatest satisfaction in the work you do?

_____

_____

_____

What value does this combination of skills, behaviors, values, and achievements help you bring to your target employers?

_____

_____

_____

_____

Now compile endorsements. Looking at each of your major areas of responsibility throughout your work history, write down any positive verbal or written commentary that others have made on your performance.

_____

_____

_____

_____

After rereading your answers, make three one-sentence statements that capture the essence of your competitive difference.

1. _____

2. _____

3. _____

Take these three statements and rework them into one sentence. This is your competitive difference.

_____

_____

_____

Making Use of Your Competitive Difference

Your answers to the CDQ are the component parts and expression of your brand. You captured the major building blocks of your current *professional brand* in three one-sentence statements, and then you captured the essence of your competitive difference in a single fourth sentence.

These statements should embody all that is best about the *professional you,* and the *spirit* of these differentiators should be evident in the consistent messaging found in your social media profiles, your resume, and in everything you do in the execution of your professional duties.

Simply understanding the *transferable skills and professional values* that underlie professional success and then completing the CDQ can change your attitude, behavior, and performance at work. Likewise, in conversation with recruiters and hiring managers, awareness of your competitive difference can infuse your whole approach and demeanor with the *special sauce* you bring to everything you do.

Are You Worth Branding Yet?

What you do with the final result of the CDQ takes real objectivity. You may look at your results and say, "Well, it's a beginning, but if this is the best I've got to say right now, maybe I shouldn't be making too much of a fuss until I have developed further in some of these areas." It is much better to come to this *emotionally mature* decision and engage yourself in developing the *transferable skills and professional values* that underlie a valid brand and help build your reputation.

Honesty in Advertising

A couple of years ago a large soft-drink manufacturer that made a "healthy" drink was sued. It turned out that the so-called healthy drink wasn't, in fact, any healthier than a regular soft drink, but consumers were fooled into buying it. Once the truth came out, however, nobody bought it again.

In the same way that a commercial brand has to deliver on its promises, you have to deliver on the promises associated with your brand. If not, you'll be very quickly found out and your job won't be the only thing you'll lose. Your reputation will be injured, perhaps irreparably, and you'll lose credibility, which is central to your professional success. Make your brand truthful; work hard to improve those parts of it that are weak and strengthen those that are outstanding. The benefits are incalculable.

Integrating a Professional Brand Signature Into Social Media Profiles

Once your competitive difference statement is polished to the point that it is valid and powerful, you might think of using it as a brand signature in your social media profiles. All four of your final CDQ answers can resonate throughout your social media profiles and resume, and the final statement—the essence of your *professional brand*—can be especially powerful as an opening statement that captures who you are and what you do.

Headline and Brand Statement

Your social media profile, followed by a brand statement, gives the reader a focus for what to expect in your profile. The brand statement is a short phrase that defines what you will bring to this job. Brand statements often start with action verbs—"Poised to," "Delivers," "Dedicated to," "Brings," "Positioned to," etc.—but only when word count allows. If it doesn't, stick to the keywords most likely to be used in searches, and place your brand statement at the beginning of your Profile Summary. For example, if you look at my LinkedIn profile, you'll see that my headline shamelessly plugs our professional resume-writing service. Then my brand statement—"Doctors save lives, I make them worth living."—is the opening statement of my summary. Here is a selection of brand statements that would be suitable for use in both your social media profiles and your resume.

Senior Operations / Plant Management Professional
"Dedicated to continuous improvement ~ Lean Six Sigma ~ Start-up & turnaround operations ~ Mergers & change management ~ Process & productivity optimization ~ Logistics & supply chain"

Account Management / Client Communications Manager
"Reliably achieving performance improvement and compliance within financial services industry"

Administrative / Office Support Professional
"Ready, willing, and competent: detail-oriented problem solver, consistently forges effective working relationships with all publics"

We'll go into greater detail about profile creation in following chapters.

Your Professional Brand and a Long Career

This packaging and positioning of the *professional you* goes beyond this particular job search. Part and parcel of achieving long-term career success is establishing credibility and a gradually increasing visibility within your department, your company, your local professional community, and perhaps ultimately your profession on a national or international level. Your steadily evolving brand—shared through social media—and your professional day-to-day conduct reinforce your growing credibility and visibility. A commitment to building your capabilities over time is *enlightened self-interest* in an insecure professional world. Change is constant in everyone's career, so while we talk about developing an initial *professional brand* as part of your job search strategy, it isn't "mission accomplished" once you've landed a new job.

Always think of your ongoing commitment to building professional capabilities and credibility as being at the heart of your career management strategies, leading to greater credibility and visibility. This continual professional development—signposted by your brand—is what keeps you current and respected in your job market.

Now that you know how to build and shape a brand, it's time to look at how to deploy that brand in building your social media profiles on the major social networking sites.

PART II

Building Your
Social Networks

CHAPTER 4

SOCIAL NETWORKING IN JOB SEARCH AND CAREER MANAGEMENT

Developing and learning to manage your social media presence is one of the greatest tools for taking control of your professional destiny. Learn to take advantage of employers' Internet-based recruitment tactics with a powerfully branded message across multiple social media sites, and your career will flourish; fail to stay current with the times, and you will be relegated to professional obscurity.

We have transformed so quickly into a digitally connected world that not having a social media profile, or even the right kind of social media profile, will work against you. With increasing frequency, professionals in the recruitment community are becoming suspicious of people without a digital footprint. I can foresee a time very soon when the lack of a cohesive social media presence will make you invisible to corporate recruiters.

How Recruitment Affects Networking Strategy

Understanding how companies recruit will help you apply productive networking tactics to every aspect of your job search, integrate these same networking tactics into your professional life in ways that will increase your job stability, credibility, and visibility in your profession, and give you the tools to better pursue entrepreneurial opportunity and the dreams that put juice in your life.

Recruitment strategy is obsessed with economy, speed, and value. The cost of hiring and training a new employee can run to more than ten thousand dollars, so the entire recruitment process is cost and productivity conscious. Consequently, the people involved in a specific search—the hiring manager, HR, and recruitment professionals—all want the same thing: good hires, fast hires, and cheap hires. The way they achieve this is logical, and understanding it can enhance your job search strategies with new tactics to quadruple the number of interviews you get (see Chapter 17 for more).

Step #1: Internal Promotions

Put yourself on the other side of the hiring manager's desk for a few moments. When looking to fill a position, you would obviously start the recruitment process by asking yourself, your peers, and your staff who within the company can do this job. Naturally, you want to hire from within, because it's cheap, you are dealing with known quantities, and internal promotions are motivational.

Step #2: Who Do You Know?

When a hiring manager can't make an internal hire, she will logically ask, "Who do I know, and who do my people know?" Recruiters will review all the resumes in the company's database and will recall any promising candidates who have been picked up on their social media radar—the world's greatest gift to employee recruitment, which in turn makes it your greatest gift as a job seeker.

HR may also create an internal job posting (often tied to cash incentives for employee referrals) and actively consider people known to employees and the recruitment team, or who can be found through their involvement in social networks. These will include contacts made through online social networks and professional and alumni associations.

Step #3: Recruitment Advertising

It is only when these first two attempts yield no results that companies begin advertising job openings. Headhunters come into use only when all else fails, and as urgency or confidentiality dictates. But even when companies progress to advertising and using headhunters, they still prefer to hire people who come to them directly or through referral networks. For you, this means that *the most effective job search tactic is networking*, a skill that, once learned, will serve you throughout your career.

Nothing happens in a job search without conversation, so much so that the prime focus of a job search should be to get into conversation with recruiters and hiring managers as quickly and frequently as possible. The people who land jobs fastest and with greatest ease are the people who are connected to their professions through social networking, because networking enables them to jump-start those all-important conversations with recruiters and hiring authorities. Follow their lead by integrating the networking strategies discussed in this book and you will be better equipped to find work in any economic climate. Conversely, jobs will become increasingly hard to find for seekers who ignore social networking. Lacking a presence where recruiters are investing their time, these professionals will become quite simply invisible.

How to Develop Professionally Relevant Networks

If you are involved in a job search right now, the quickest way to get past the living hell of the experience is to *get into conversations as quickly and as frequently as possible with the people who can hire you*—and the people who *know* and *work with* the people who can hire you.

The most effective way to make this happen is to build and maintain networks that are relevant to your professional needs. The better connected you are to your professional community, the more visible you become. Building social networks that better connect you to your professional community makes it easier for recruiters and hiring managers to find you, and easier for you to reach out to these same recruiters and managers.

When you connect with your professional community and build professionally relevant networks, you get to know and be known by all the most dedicated and best-connected professionals—in your target location at first, and, with experience and seniority, perhaps nationally and globally.

The Importance of Profession-Relevant Networks

Most people rush to build networks when they are changing jobs and realize how few people they know and how poorly connected they are to their professional community. There is a lesson to be learned from this: In an increasingly uncertain world, you need to build social networks for this job search and maintain those networks once you land that next job on your professional path. This keeps you visible both within your professional community and among the corporate recruiters and headhunters who may call you down the road with unexpected opportunities. You don't have to accept them, but isn't it better to have a network that delivers knowledge of the opportunities, and the privilege of accepting or rejecting them as you see fit, as opposed to never hearing about them?

Additionally, next time you plan a job change you will have a larger and more mature network to help you plan and execute the change on *your* timetable. You plant the seeds when you initiate a new relationship, but you don't harvest the best fruit immediately. Networking can and does bear fruit right away, but your harvest will get richer over time as you become more adept at networking and nurturing your networking contacts.

Types of Networks

There are more networking options than you will ever have time to cultivate unless social networking becomes your profession, so you'll need to put all the networks we discuss through your personal filters to judge which ones will be most helpful to you. Your goal should be to integrate networking into your life so that it is not a chore. If you haven't started to make this transition yet, you will be surprised how easy it can be.

There are four types of networks that can contribute to the success of job search and the larger issues of career management:

1. Online social networking and offline meet-ups
2. Online and offline professional associations
3. Online and offline alumni networks
4. Online and offline community networks

We will address each of these networks in turn, and discuss how best to leverage your involvement with them. Networks grow in value over time and in direct proportion to your ongoing nurturing of them; the longer you have networks in each of these categories, the more helpful they will become in helping you achieve your goals and weather life's storms.

Online Social Networking

For you, social networks provide a reliable pathway to millions of jobs through the people connected to them, while for hiring managers, corporate recruiters, and headhunters, social networking sites are honey pots, offering millions of qualified candidates all in one place. Social networking is a win/win proposition, a boon regardless of the side of the hiring desk on which you sit.

The more connected you are with other professionals in your area of expertise, the greater your odds of gaining referrals to jobs in the hidden job market. The connections you make can also lead to referrals and introductions to hiring managers, and in instances where you've seen a job posting, network contacts can help you bypass the job sites and their resume banks entirely.

You can search a social networking site's database by zip code, job title, company, or any keywords of your choice. The database will pull up the profiles of people who match your requirements and allow you to initiate contact directly, through your common membership in groups, or through the chain of people who connect you.

To see how this works, let's take for example a soldier cycling out of the military, who sought my help in her search for a new civilian career. Not only was she changing jobs, she was also engaged in the greater challenge of career change—from the military to the civilian world. I took her to *www.LinkedIn.com*. First, to find other individuals with a similar background, I plugged the word *army* into the dialogue box and hit enter. The result was more than one million profiles of people who shared her military experience. We then tried a search using the phrase *information technology* (reflecting her desired career change) and got 176,000 profiles. While both these potential networks would have relevance to her job search, it got even better when we combined the keywords *information technology* and *army*. This pulled up a slightly more manageable 94,000 people who shared her life experience, many of whom had already made a similar transition from army into information technology, while many of the rest worked in military applications of information technology. This meant that she had identified thousands of people who shared her specific life experiences and professional interests, greatly increasing the odds of productive conversations with an enormous number of people, all of whom were prequalified as likely to have some useful advice for her job search. Similar results are awaiting you.

Which Social Networks Are Right for You?

In the coming chapters we will look at how to get the best results from LinkedIn, Google+, Facebook, and Twitter, the four biggest social networking sites, which are also the sites most used by recruiters, headhunters, and hiring managers.

I suggest that you begin by developing a profile on LinkedIn that reflects the *professional persona* you want to show the world, then duplicate it on Google+. Subsequently, you can tweak your Facebook profile to ensure that your messaging is perhaps more casual, but nevertheless consistent. Following this, it can pay to learn how to use Twitter in your job search. Twitter, of the four major social networking sites, also has unique capabilities as a career management tool, enabling you to quickly share profession-relevant information that enhances your credibility and visibility once you land your next job.

Social networking can be addictive, and it is easy to fool yourself into thinking that you are working with purpose when in reality you are acting like a four-year-old let loose in a room full of colorful bouncing balls. Social media sites, and websites in general, are designed to keep you clicking and wanting more, more, more. Because all social media sites are distracting, the way you manage the social networking aspect of your job search and your life in general needs to be focused.

Specialty Networking Sites

It is more productive to learn to use one or two social media platforms well than it is to use a dozen badly. We have limited space here and will concentrate on the leading four social networking sites. However, if you are a linguist, a social media site for the multilingual might prove useful, because in a global economy people with language skills have a special edge. Consequently, social networking sites that attract multilingual professionals will also attract recruiters from any company searching for language and multicultural awareness skills in new employees. The same applies if you belong to any kind of recognized minority: There is probably a social media group for you that is haunted by recruiters looking for the technical skills and the "special sauce" your particular minority status brings to the table. For a comprehensive listing of social media sites you can go to *www.en.wikipedia .org/wiki/List_of_social_networks*.

The Confidential Job Search

When you are employed and engaged in a confidential job search, a properly constructed social media profile will make you discoverable, and because a social networking site is not a resume bank, you do it without an "I'm for sale" sign.

Most social networking sites allow you to customize your settings and say whom you would like to hear from and what you would like to hear about; "job opportunities" will always be included in the options. When you are currently employed and conducting a confidential job search, checking this box can only cause problems with your current employer. Fortunately, not checking the box will never discourage a recruiter who wants to speak to you, so don't worry about not announcing that you are looking for new opportunities.

In the next chapter, we'll look at how to reverse engineer a job description to help you create powerful social media profiles that will be readily discoverable by recruiters and resonate with their needs.

CHAPTER 5

How to Create a Discoverable Social Media Profile

The first thing a recruiter or hiring manager hears about you is whatever they read on your social media profile and resume. In this chapter, we'll take a unique look at how to reverse engineer your target customers' job descriptions to discover what employers in your profession think is most important—how they think about, express, and prioritize their needs. The insights you gain into how employers, *your customers*, think—and the skills, behaviors, and values that are important to them—will enable you to create social media profiles that are not only discoverable, but which also resonate with their needs, because they will reflect the priorities and language employers use.

A Killer Social Media Profile

The first business lesson you learned was: "The customer is always right." The second lesson was: "Find out what the customers want and sell it to them." Yet when most people come to create their social media profiles and resume, for some reason they tend to skip the step of analyzing customer needs, relying instead on what they *think* is important.

Your social media profiles (and matching resume) are the most financially important documents you will ever own. When they work, you work. When they don't work, you don't either, so building your social networks on firm foundations is a priority that deserves your full attention, especially when your work can do double duty as the basis for a resume that carries the same messaging, priorities, and tone. This reverse engineering process will help you establish achievable goals for your search and open the doors of opportunity for interviews. The increased self-awareness you gain from connecting employer needs with your skills and achievements will even prepare you for job interviews and the questions interviewers will likely ask.

A social media profile is not simply a recitation of all the things you have done in your work life. In fact, if it just lists all the things you happen to think are important, it will probably be undiscoverable. The major social media sites—LinkedIn, Google+, Facebook, and Twitter—all have more than 200 million members; some exceed the billion mark. In this world, an ill-conceived social media profile will never be found; it will be a minnow in an ocean of millions of other minnows that all look just the same. It will remain undiscovered and unread.

Foundations of a Discoverable Social Media Profile

Many social media profiles simply don't work for their owners because they haven't been thought through and built properly. A profile that crams in everything you have ever done without any real focus will be far less discoverable than a profile built on careful analysis of customer priorities.

When recruiters are searching on social networking sites, they do so with a specific Job Description (JD) in mind. Because job postings usually reflect the exact wording of the JDs they come from, this means that you can get an insight into exactly how employers think about and prioritize the needs for your target job by analyzing the posting, enabling you to identify the priorities and the words and phrases that employers use when they are looking for someone like you.

Understanding Employer Priorities

Understanding exactly how employers think about, prioritize, and express their needs for the job you need to land will give you objective criteria to guide the development of your social media profiles. I have devised a tool that will do this called Target Job Deconstruction (TJD). It will give you:

- A template for the story that your social media profile (and resume) *must* tell to be successful
- The examples and achievements to illustrate the claims of your profile
- An objective tool against which to evaluate your profile's likely performance
- An understanding of interviewers' likely focus at interviews
- A good idea of the questions that will be heading your way and why
- Relevant examples with which to illustrate your answers
- A behavioral profile for getting hired and for professional success throughout your career
- A behavioral profile for not getting hired and for ongoing professional failure

Once you have this focus, you can look backward into your professional history for those experiences that best position you for the target job.

Target Job Deconstruction (TJD)

Step #1: Decide on a Primary Target Job

Some people think you change jobs to get a promotion, but this is largely incorrect, especially in a tight job market. *People get hired based on their credentials, not their potential.* Typically, most professionals accept a position similar to the one they have now, but one that offers opportunity for growth once they have proved themselves.

Focus on a specific and realistic target job, one in which you can succeed based on the skills you possess today. This will be:

- A job you can do
- A job for which you can make a convincing argument with your social media profiles and resume
- A job you can convince skilled interviewers that you can do
- A job in which you can succeed

Let's look at "a job in which you can succeed." Seventy percent of the requested skills/experience will usually get you into the running for the selection cycle in any economy. In your search for jobs, don't throw out opportunities just because one line in the job description speaks of skills you lack. If you meet the 70 percent guideline, you are a worthy candidate. Less than this and you may need to reconsider your target job or anticipate a longer job search to reach your goals.

If you have more than five years of experience, there are probably a couple of jobs you can do. More than fifteen years' experience and there could be half a dozen jobs in which you could succeed. Carefully evaluate and rank these jobs based on their availability, remuneration, fulfillment, and potential for growth or shrinkage. This way you will target a "primary job" based on practicality and common sense. Settle on the one that will be *the easiest sell for you and the easiest buy for the employer.*

If you ultimately decide you want to go after that White Water Rafting Guide job because you once owned a canoe . . . well, at least you'll be doing it with your eyes open, knowing that you won't have most of the required skills and that your search will take considerably longer.

This does not mean you cannot pursue any of those other jobs for which you have the desire or some of the qualifications. However, you are best served by being sensible and creating a profile with a single "primary target job." Because social media profiles can be more detailed than resumes, by all means add the details of the other jobs you can do within the body of your profile—just don't let them obscure the primary focus.

Step #2: Collect Job Postings

Next, collect six postings for your chosen primary target job. If you want to save some time, try one of the job aggregators, or spiders (so-called because they *crawl* the web looking for suitable jobs based on your search criteria), listed below, each of which will search thousands of job sites and employers for you:

- *www.indeed.com*
- *www.SimplyHired.com*
- *www.jobbankusa.com*
- *www.jobster.com*

Most are free, and most also have fee-based services; for this exercise the free services will be quite adequate. The home page on each of these sites invariably has a couple of dialogue boxes: one for a job title and one for a geographic area. If you cannot find half a dozen jobs in your target location, just try another major metropolitan area or leave the second box empty—for the purpose of TJD, it really doesn't matter where the jobs are located.

Step #3: Look at Your Target Job from the Other Side of the Desk

This is where you start to deconstruct your six job postings to develop an understanding of exactly how employers *think about, prioritize, and describe the deliverables of your target job*:

1. Open a new MS Word document.
2. Under a subhead of "Target Job Titles," cut and paste all the variations on the job title from your six job postings.
3. Add a second subhead entitled:

   "Experience/Responsibilities/Skills/Deliverables/Etc."

   Review your collection of job postings and find *one* requirement that is common to all six job postings. Choose the most complete description of that particular requirement and paste it under the second subhead, then put the number 6 in front of it to signify that it is common to all six job postings.

   Next, revisit the other five postings looking for additional keywords used to describe this same requirement. When you find an alternative word or phrase, post it beneath the requirement description that you chose.

   Repeat this step for any other requirements that are common to all six of your collected job postings, placing the number 6 alongside each one.
4. Repeat this process with requirements that are common to five of the job postings, then four . . . and so on down the

line until you finally come to requirements that only appear on one job posting.

At the end of this first part of the TJD process, you will be able to read the document and say to yourself, *"When employers are looking for _____, these are the job titles they use; this is the order in which their needs are prioritized, these are the skills, experiences, deliverables, and professional behaviors they look for, and these are the words with which they describe the deliverables of the job."*

As you read through your TJD document, the story your social media profile (and resume) must tell will be clearly laid out before you.

Step #4: Identify What's Missing

In some companies, especially bigger ones, JDs can be maddeningly vague because they all have to be approved by the Legal Department before they see the light of day. This is part of an overall corporate cost-containment policy designed to protect against the release of JDs that might aid individual or class-action lawsuits brought by disgruntled employees. How can I be sure of this? I used to be a director of human resources in Silicon Valley; I've overseen this process.

There are plenty of job descriptions that don't tell the whole story, so add to your TJD any additional skills/experiences that you believe are relevant to this job.

If you are new to the professional world and cannot bring personal awareness of a job's needs to the TJD process, you might want to do a little additional research to ensure that your resume has the proper focus. One way to do this is to visit the Occupational Outlook Handbook pages at *www.bls.gov/ooh/home.htm*, which give detailed analyses of hundreds of jobs.

Then for further insight into a specific target job, join profession-relevant groups on LinkedIn and ask questions about key responsibilities. Be respectful and show appreciation for advice given, and you will not only get the information you need about the daily responsibilities of the target job, you will begin to develop one of your professional networks. We'll discuss approaches to group interaction a little later in the book.

Step #5: Problem Solving

At their most elemental level, all jobs are the same—they all focus on *problem identification, prevention, and solution.* This is what we all get paid for, no matter what the job title. So we need to think about the *problem identification, prevention, and solution* challenges presented by each of the job's requirements.

Armed with this insight, go back to your TJD and, starting with the first requirement, think about and note the problems you will typically need to *identify, prevent, and/or solve* in the course of a normal work day as you deliver on this requirement of the job. Then list specific examples, big and small, of your successful *identification, prevention, and/or solution of those problems.* Quantify your results when possible.

Repeat this with each of the TJD's other requirements by identifying the problems inherent in that particular responsibility. Some of the examples you recall may appear in your social media profile as significant professional achievements; these, and others you choose not to use on your social media profiles, will give you good ammunition for all those interview questions that begin, "Tell me about a time when . . ."

Step #6: Achievements

Make a list of your greatest solo professional achievements for each of your identified job priorities, quantifying the results where you can, to demonstrate the value of your work. This can and should include both personal achievement and team achievements to which you contributed.

Step #7: A Behavioral Profile for Success

Have you ever thought about the behavioral profile that defines success in your area of expertise, and then measured yourself against it? Doing so can help you define the professional you want to be and the persona you want to show to the professional world. Not understanding how your behavior can help or hinder your success usually means that you are unwittingly sabotaging future potential.

Additionally, interviewers always have an image of the person they want to hire. This is not about height, weight, and hair color; it's a mental behavioral composite of the best people they've seen doing this job and it's what managers will hire when they find.

Work your way through each of the responsibilities itemized in your TJD one by one, profiling the *best* person you ever saw doing that aspect of the job and what made her stand out. Describe how she went about the work, skills hard and soft, interaction with others, general attitude and demeanor, and anything else that sticks out in your mind about that person, and you'll get something like: *Carole Jenkins, superior communication skills, always asking questions and listening, a fine analytical mind, great professional appearance, and a nice person to work with; she'd do anything for anyone.* Do this for each one of the job's deliverables and you will have a detailed behavioral profile of the person all employers want to hire and everyone wants as a colleague. Additionally, you have just created a behavioral blueprint for your own professional success.

Step #8: A Behavioral Profile for Failure

Just as interviewers always have an image of the person they want to hire, they also know the type of person they want to avoid;

this profile is a behavioral composite of the worst people they've had doing this job, and it's what managers want to avoid at all costs. Now, revisiting each of the TJD's prioritized requirements again, this time think of the *worst* person you have ever worked with in that area of responsibility and what made that individual stand out in such a negative way. Describe the performance, professional behaviors, interaction with others, and general attitude and demeanor of that person and you'll get something like: *Jack Dornitz, insecure, critical, passive aggressive, and no social graces.* At the end of this step you will have a description of the person that all employers want to avoid and the person that no one wants to work with: *You will also have a behavioral profile for long periods of unemployment, and ultimately career failure.* Once this is done, compare yourself to this profile and see if there is anything you need to change or work on.

Step #9: Transferable Skills and Professional Values

The final step of the TJD is to review each of the prioritized requirements one last time to identify which of the *transferable skills and professional values* help you execute your responsibilities in each of the prioritized responsibilities. How often these skills and values are repeated in your review will help determine which are your strongest assets and which may need some development.

Once you complete and review your TJD, you will have a clear idea of the way employers prioritize, think about, and express their needs for your target job. You'll know what they'll ask about at interviews and, beyond the hard skills, you'll understand the behavioral profile of the person they will hire.

The TJD exercise will take a little time and it would be easy to cut corners or just skip it, but this is your career and this is your life, and it isn't brain surgery. Make the effort and invest in your long-term success and happiness.

The immediate results of your work will be a template for the story your social media profiles *and* resume need to tell, and an objective tool against which to evaluate the documents you create. This will result in social media profiles that are discoverable. A little further down the road, when you are settled in a new job, you can apply what you have learned from the behavioral profile for success to your daily professional life, and you will increase your job security and opportunities as your networking documents open doors to the inner circles that exist in every department and company.

In the next chapter, we'll look at how to build a *Knock 'em Dead* social media profile for LinkedIn, the world's premier networking site—a profile that you can then easily customize for Google+, Facebook, and Twitter, the other major social networking sites we'll discuss in subsequent chapters.

CHAPTER 6

LinkedIn

By far the most important networking site for professionals is LinkedIn. Use it correctly and it could well help you land your next job and sustain your future professional growth. While the following discussion is focused on how best to leverage your presence on LinkedIn, you should be aware that most social networking sites function in very similar ways, and many topics we discuss in this chapter will apply to the other networking sites you join.

When you first join a networking site, your goals are twofold: You want to be discoverable by recruiters and you want to develop professional connections that can help you with your job search and perhaps with the more general issues of career management. With LinkedIn, as with any social networking site, there are certain steps to take that help you get the most out of the social networking experience:

- Register and create a profile: This gives you a presence so that others can find and connect with you.
- Connect with everyone you know or have worked with in the past.

- Expand your network by joining special interest groups that are relevant to your profession, and connect with members whose acquaintance could prove mutually beneficial; more on the specifics of who to connect with shortly.
- Join job search groups for mutual support and tactics. There are many groups; one of them is the *Knock 'em Dead Secrets & Strategies* group: It's a friendly, vibrant group that exists to help you with job search and career management issues.
- Link with me, which will immediately increase your reach by thousands.
- Engage in social networking activities that will increase your visibility and attract others to you.

All this begins with creating a profile.

How to Create a Killer LinkedIn Profile

LinkedIn exists to provide professional networking opportunities for members. All social networking sites are attractive to recruiters, but LinkedIn is the honey pot for recruiters, and you are the honey. Your first step is to create a profile that will make you visible and attractive to these recruiters and to the professional peers who will be looking for you, just as you are looking for them.

There are now well over 300 million LinkedIn users (half of them in the United States) and the site is growing daily, so building a profile that helps you stand out from the crowd will pay real dividends. Because it is also increasingly common for recruiters and hiring managers to check out your social media profile(s) once they have seen your resume, the profile you create will give you greater visibility with search engines, and enable recruiters and others to find you from outside of LinkedIn.

It All Starts with Your Headshot

Your headshot appears at the top left of your LinkedIn profile, and it's the first thing recruiters—or anyone else—who visits your profile (or merely discovers it in a list of search results) sees. Upward of 90 percent of Human Resources pros say they check out social media profiles, especially LinkedIn and Facebook, before inviting a candidate in for an interview. As the face you show to the world, your headshot is the face of your brand.

This means the wrong headshot could hurt your chances of making the cut. Five out of every ten social media profile headshots make me want to laugh, cry, or lose my lunch. I see headshots that are too close (you want to minimize wrinkles or acne), too far (I need to see your face), too sexy, too casual, grinning like a congenital imbecile, or scowling like a mass murderer. These problem headshots show a lack of appreciation for how important this first impression really is.

Every Picture Tells a Story

Headshots aren't just for celebrities anymore; they have become a critically important part of establishing a credible professional image for all of us. Like it or not, your headshot tells a story, so make sure yours is telling the right story.

We all make judgments based on visual first impressions; with search results, a profile with a headshot will get many more clicks than a profile without one, and the people who come to your profile will form an opinion based on your headshot before they read anything you have written. How professional and accessible your headshot makes you look will also color the impressions of anyone who then reads your profile. It's safe to say that getting your headshot right is extremely important.

Are You Trying to Get Hired or Dated?

We all have different personas at work and at play, so a killer headshot for your Match.com profile could be the kiss of death for your LinkedIn profile. Your social media profile gives the reader visual clues as to who you are and what your self-image is. Your appearance and facial expression provide the clues, and these are communicated through your headshot. It will happen whether you want it to or not, so the only smart choice is to make sure your headshot presents a confident professional. If you're seen as both professional (which implies competence) and friendly, you will encourage acceptance of the claims made within your profile, whereas a too casual or too sexy shot will call your judgment of professional issues into question.

Can You Get Away with a DIY Headshot?

As long as you look professional, the headshot doesn't have to be done by a professional, but headshots aren't snapshots and you should dress for yours as you would for a job interview.

You can probably get a friend/lover/partner to shoot a bunch of photos of you against a plain background and it will come out as an acceptable candid shot. Since we all need these shots in our professional lives, a competent headshot photography partner should be easy to find.

The beauty of a digital camera is that you can take as many shots as you want, pick the best one, and maybe even do some basic cleanups. Shoot straight on and then experiment with distance. Once you've settled on a distance (between four and eight feet for many cameras), experiment with angles to see which is most flattering; adjust the lighting to get the most complimentary result.

You need the best headshot you can generate for immediate use, but bear in mind that summer is the best time to upgrade your social media headshots: You look happier and more relaxed because it's summer, and for paler skins any kind of tan makes you look healthier and more attractive.

Your Headline

After your headshot, the next thing recruiters notice is your headline. This headline should say who you are and what you do; it is important to give recruiters focus, and this is one of the areas the search engine rates as important in establishing your ranking in searches. (Ensuring that your ranking in searches is high is called search engine optimization or SEO.) This headline is limited to a 120-character thumbnail description about you and works as a brief biography of the person behind the headshot. You have just these 120 characters to say who you are, so your headline should include your Target Job Title and the keywords that most succinctly capture what you do. You might consider the branding statements you established as your professional special sauce at the end of the CDQ discussed in Chapter 3. You increase the odds of these working well by doing searches on LinkedIn for your own target job title and looking at how the people who show up on the first few pages of results build a winning headline. Use this insight to adapt what you have to offer to synchronize with your findings.

A First- or Third-Person Voice?

While your resume usually uses a third-person voice, a social media profile has evolved as a longer, more revealing, and personal document, so you want to write both conversationally and concisely. If you have read *Knock 'em Dead Resume Templates*, you know that the easiest way to create the body of your profile is to upload your resume into the appropriate section and convert it to a first-person voice. This is possible because *Knock 'em Dead* resumes are built to address the same issues as social media profiles and achieve the highest visibility.

Summary

This should include information that will maximize your *discoverability* when a recruiter searches for someone like you. Information in your Summary section should be geared to drawing a concise picture of your professional capabilities—not your hopes and dreams but your *capabilities*, because you get hired based on your credentials, not your potential.

The summary on your LinkedIn profile (as on other social networking sites) provides more space than you would usually use in the Summary or Performance Profile section of a job-targeted resume. However, if you have already built a resume according to *Knock 'em Dead* guidelines, you will have a Performance Profile that reflects the skills, experience, priorities, and word choices employers use to define the job they need to fill. If so, just upload the resume and change it to a first-person voice. If you *don't* have a *Knock 'em Dead* resume, identify the raw materials for the Summary in your TJD exercises (see Chapter 5) and then write six sentences that succinctly capture your capabilities in each of the employer priority areas.

The summary and work experience sections of your LinkedIn profile accommodate a considerable word count. However, anything you write needs to be accessible to the human eye, and long blocks of text become visually inaccessible very quickly, especially to recruiters who are scanning briefly rather than reading. Consequently, you need to make sure that no paragraph is more than six lines of unbroken text. You can also use bullet points to share important information and deliver visual variety.

Some career "experts" suggest writing about your hobbies here. That's silly. No recruiter cares about your personal interests until they know you can do the job, so such information is irrelevant to recruiters, a waste of this valuable selling space, and will cost you readers. Besides, LinkedIn has provided a space for this, where it belongs: at the *end* of your profile.

Instead, use any remaining available space to list critically important skill sets for your work. There is a place for peer-reviewed professional skills later, but listing them here is very helpful to recruiters, and you certainly won't diminish the discoverability of your profile by mentioning these skills more than once.

Work Experience

The experience section of your profile begins with your current job and work experience. Again, you can cut and paste the entry from your resume first, then add to this with additional information that you feel is relevant.

Review your entries to see if there is additional experience you would like to add. You have plenty of space here, so as long as your headline and entries for each job start with the most important information as determined by your TJD—making your profile more discoverable and a more tempting read for recruiters—you can continue to add additional supporting information until you run out of space.

Whatever you do, don't be lazy and just list your current job: That gives the impression that you have only had the one. LinkedIn will tell you that you're twelve times more likely to be found by recruiters when you have more than one job listed—perhaps because those other jobs allow you to weight your profile with enough relevant keywords in each job's headline to increase your discoverability in recruiters' database searches.

The inclusion of keywords in each job's headline and in the details of that work experience helps make you more visible. This helps recruiters see your claims of professional competency in context and will dramatically increase the frequency of keyword usage. Do this with each job and your discoverability will steadily rise in the results of recruiters' searches.

Skills

LinkedIn has a Skills area that allows you to identify up to fifty different skills. Using your Target Job Deconstruction document to determine the skills your customers seek in someone with your professional title, you should add a list of professional skills to your LinkedIn profile.

Skill Endorsements

Once your profile is visible to the public, people can endorse you for each of these skills (a favor you can initiate and return). The more endorsements you have of your skills, the more discoverable you become to recruiters. Adding skills to your LinkedIn profile has the same benefits as adding it to your resume: It makes your profile more visible in database searches and your skills more readily accessible to readers.

You can post up to fifty skills in the dialogue box; however, you will also want your contacts to endorse you for these skills, so listing fewer skills can mean more endorsements for each, and more endorsements help your discoverability. As your networks grow, they'll certainly include others who are in transition, and mutual skill endorsements can help you both.

Education

Start with your highest educational level and work backward. While your educational attainments will usually stop with post-secondary education in your resume, with a LinkedIn profile you might want to consider listing high school as well: This increases your networking opportunities. Just a week before the time of writing, I personally received a connect request from a high school friend living half a world away, whom I'd lost touch with many years ago.

Certifications

Add all your professional certifications; they demonstrate that either your employers, or you personally, have seen fit to invest in your ongoing professional education. They also speak to money that a new employer doesn't have to invest. Additionally, they can be used by recruiters as search terms, making you more discoverable.

Interests

Finally, here is the place where it is appropriate to add information about your outside interests! If someone has read this far, learning that I enjoy history, historical fiction, kayaking, ballroom dancing, rock 'n roll, mixed media art, collecting acoustic phonographs, Prohibition-era cocktail shakers, and art-deco chrome; am the world's worst bass player; and enjoy tinkering with stuff around the garden can offer new ways of seeing me as a real person, rather than just a set of skills.

While earlier in the profile this information would only be a distraction, here, toward the end, it can add depth and encourage an image of you as a living, breathing human being. Even if a recruiter isn't interested in your human side, the fact that you waited until the end of your profile to convey such information means that it won't take away from anyone's perception of your professional competence.

Associations and Awards

Include membership in any associations or societies, as these are also search terms a recruiter might use, on the assumption that people who belong to professional associations are, by definition, likely to be more committed to—and therefore more up-to-date with—the *technical skills* of their profession.

Reading List

Be sure your list includes profession-oriented materials, because the target audiences you want to impress are recruiters and hiring managers.

Spelling, Punctuation, and Grammar

The same considerations you apply to spelling, punctuation, and grammar in your resume or any other professional document destined for worldwide publication also apply here. If you have problems creating your profile or editing it, you can get help at *Knock 'em Dead* Resume Services, where we create LinkedIn profiles for our clients and also offer a separate social networking profile copyediting service, similar to the one we offer for resumes.

Recommendations

LinkedIn likes your profile to have at least three recommendations, and doesn't recognize it as complete until you do. This is in your best interests too, as recommendations from colleagues, coworkers, and past managers give your profile depth and increase your appeal to recruiters. The easiest way to get recommendations is to do them for your colleagues and then ask them to reciprocate. LinkedIn will send a recommendation to the recipient and ask him (a) if he would like to upload it, and (b) if he would like to reciprocate. If he doesn't reciprocate within a couple of days, send a personal request. You don't need to tell someone he *owes* you a reference in return for yours, just that you'd appreciate it.

If you are returning to the workforce after an absence, you can use recommendations from volunteer work. Also, you can reach out to people who gave you written recommendations and ask them to be duplicated on LinkedIn. You can make things easier by sending such people an e-mail with a copy of the recommendation.

Link Your Resume to Your Social Media Profile

Once your profile is complete and supports the story told in your resume, upload the resume as directed. Linking to your resume is useful because a resume is still the most succinct vehicle for sharing your professional skills, and recruiters will use it for their records and to review with hiring managers. Your resume in turn should have a mutual link to your LinkedIn profile (beneath your hyperlinked e-mail address), so that HR or the hiring manager can click through and gather more insight into your potential candidacy.

Privacy and Saving Your Work

Building your profile may take a week before you have it exactly right, so you should know that every time you change a sentence on your LinkedIn profile and log out, LinkedIn can automatically send a change of status to your network. As you may make many changes to get it right, you don't want your contacts notified every few minutes. To avoid this, do three things:

1. Write your early drafts on a Word document with headings that match the site's profile subject headers. Then make changes to your heart's content without any danger of unwittingly sharing your edits with the world. When you do upload, you'll invariably still want to tweak your copy and so still want to maintain privacy.
2. Go to *Settings* from the drop-down menu under your name on the top right of your homepage and look for *Privacy Controls*. Chose *Private* while you are making profile changes. This will keep your changes private until your profile is complete and you release it for public display.
3. Save everything in the final published draft in a Microsoft Word document. This will give you a complete social media profile ready for fast adaptation when you join other

social networking sites. Back up your work, because if you don't, somewhere along the line you are going to lose it.

You can also use the *Public Profile Settings* to customize your existing LinkedIn URL to make it more attention grabbing and informative—perhaps reflecting your job title.

Search Engine Optimization (SEO) and You

At this point you have a profile ready to be optimized for maximum discoverability by search engines. LinkedIn, like all social networking sites, has specific and, annoyingly, ever-changing advice for Search Engine Optimization (SEO), so you should always check the "Help" pages to ensure that you are current. Despite this constantly changing advice, a couple of SEO-worthy actions have remained constant.

Your headline (coming next to the headshot at the top of your profile) should include your target job title and as many priority skills as space permits. The special skills you list should be those terms you think a recruiter would be most likely to use, based on your findings in the TJD exercise.

The target job title and relevant skills are always attractive to a search engine and using them increases your discoverability. So, working through your professional history, for each new job, always fill in the job title and then test how many skills, relevant to your target job, can be added before you run out of space.

Completing Your Profile

LinkedIn does not consider your profile complete until you have at least fifty connections. Therefore you should immediately reach out to anyone with whom you have connections from present or past employers, college or high school, neighbors and friends, and people you have gotten to know through either professional association or your local community. Much more advice on making profession-specific connections is coming shortly.

The Webmail Import Feature

An easy way to discover almost everyone you know who is already on LinkedIn is to use the *webmail import* feature. This will compare the webmail addresses in your e-mail program with members and tell you of people you're likely to know.

Once you have reached out to connect with all current and past colleagues, professional acquaintances, and coworkers, it is time to start expanding the depth and breadth of your network to people you don't know, but who, by virtue of their titles and where they work, you feel might be able to help you now or in the future.

The 800-Pound LinkedIn Elephant

LinkedIn's creators started out saying that you should only connect with people you already know, and they have never changed their stance, so unless they backpedal between my writing and your reading, you may well see this advice when you first join. However, the site's users have dramatically changed the way that the site is used. It is now common practice and completely allowable to connect with people you don't know and have never met. Using LinkedIn groups is one of the most effective ways to do this.

The LinkedIn Job Fairy

Sorry to be the bearer of bad news, but once you have created a LinkedIn profile (or let us create one for you), you can't just sit back and wait for the offers of job interviews to start pouring in, because there is no LinkedIn job fairy. However, once you create a discoverable profile on the most important professional networking site in the world, you can start reaching out to make connections beyond the people you already know.

LinkedIn Groups

LinkedIn only permits you to reach out to someone directly if you know each other or if you have a shared interest, and being a member of the same group counts as that shared interest. LinkedIn has thousands of special-interest groups where you can find exactly the people most likely to shape your future for the better. This makes group membership a key tool for leveraging your LinkedIn network, as it allows you to reach out and establish relationships with a very significant cross-section of your professional community. You are allowed to join up to fifty groups and can change the groups you belong to whenever you want. Joining groups that attract people from your profession should be a primary goal.

To connect with people within these groups, you can "like" someone's comment on one of the discussions (he or she will be notified and flattered) or even add your own comments. Subsequently, you can approach anyone you have complimented in this way for a connection in the following thirty-six hours—long enough not to look needy and soon enough that you'll still be remembered. You can also simply approach them for connection, based on your common interests as expressed by your mutual membership in that particular group.

Whom Do You Connect With?

Almost anyone in your industry or immediate area can be useful, regardless of title or experience, but the people of most interest, the people who, based on your professional goals, hold high-value job titles, are most valuable. They will fall into these categories:

1. *People who hold job titles that are one, two, or three levels above your own, because these are the people most likely to be in a position to hire you, now and in the future.*
2. *Those with the same job title as you, and ideally within your target industry and location.*
3. *Those people one job title below yours, and ideally within your target industry and location.*
4. *Those job titles with which you would interact on a regular basis at work. People holding these titles will have different functions and might work in different departments, but they are close enough to potentially hear of opportunities.*

People with these job titles are the people most likely to know about suitable opportunities, have the authority to hire you, or have the ability to make a referral or introduction to someone who does.

Advanced People Search

Apart from finding high-value job titles in groups, you can use the "advanced people search." You can enter job titles and identify geographic locations and/or companies with this tool and expect thousands of responses within seconds.

As people with a lot of connections are typically more active and involved with LinkedIn, go to "sort by" and look for "number of connections," then start by limiting your search to 500+ connections. Prepare a short and professional invitation, because this sector of the LI community is most likely to accept your request. You can subsequently work your way downward on the connectivity ladder. As you examine your search results in this exercise, you should also check the groups to which these people belong, which will either show a bond of interest through common group membership, or alternatively make you aware of groups that might benefit you.

Pay It Forward

You can initiate relationships by asking for advice; many people will give you a few minutes of their time, but you will develop the best relationships by reaching out to others with help and advice, because when you offer good things, forging a relationship with you becomes important to the other person.

Making Posts

You can help your growing circle of colleagues that make up the different groups you belong to just by sharing useful information—while simultaneously increasing your credibility and visibility. We are all drowning in Internet-delivered information, and whatever your profession, it is undoubtedly jammed with bloggers and curators of profession-relevant content.

One option is to identify half a dozen respected resources; for example, if you are sharing business issues, you can't go wrong linking to the *Harvard Business Review*. The mere fact that you refer to them on a regular basis (as we do on the *Knock 'em Dead* blog) is seen as evidence that you are someone who keeps abreast of the important topics in the business community with reliable commentators. All you have to do is write a post that consists of a sentence or two that say why you think such and such is interesting, and then add a link to the source. In effect, you are making intelligent posts by curating the work of others. You get points for perception but don't waste job search time writing the damn things.

An alternative is to use Google Alerts. With this option, you click on *Alerts* on Google.com and enter search terms that are of interest to you and others in your profession. Google will send you links to matching results. One word of caution: Stay away from politics, religion, and sex; they will all damage your *professional brand*. We'll discuss further tools for curating profession-relevant information over the coming chapters.

Sharing Job Leads

It's a challenge to encourage relationships that share introductions and job leads. The solution, however, is logical and painless: *Use the job leads that are inappropriate for your own use.* It's a not-so-funny thing about a job search: When you are fresh out of school, no one is hiring entry-level workers; they all want you to call back in five years. Five years later, when you are once again looking for a job, they either want someone fresh out of school or with ten years' experience.

Murphy's Law guarantees that when you are in transition, you will constantly run across positions that aren't right for you. Turn this around by using them in your networking. They could be just what someone else above or below you in the food chain is aching to hear about. Offer these leads to your connections and to others through posts on groups you belong to: "Just came across _____ jobs for _____ that aren't right for me. Anyone looking for this kind of work, please contact." This will encourage a growing network and also add connections whom you can ask to reciprocate.

When No Means of Connecting Exist

On those occasions when you discover high-value job titles but have no obvious means of connecting to them, you can send an internal message asking for permission to contact them through the people you know who *are* connected; LinkedIn shows you the connection chain and how to do this. You can use the same messaging mentioned in the prior paragraph as part of your personal request for a connection or introduction, or try this variation: "I am involved in a strategic career move right now, and I have come across a job that isn't right for me but could be perfect for you. I'll be happy to pass the lead on, and perhaps you have heard about something that would suit me. I am cycling out of the army and into the private sector and have been looking for jobs in IT in the _____ area. Any leads you think might be helpful would be welcome."

Why Build an Unwanted Jobs Database?

Build your own database of the jobs that are not suitable for you and pass them on to all those people above and below you in your profession, and you'll make lots of useful networking partners. Remember that as you progress through your career over the years, these same people are going to be moving up right along with you. Try to be helpful whenever you can over the years, and your colleagues will reciprocate. People will help you navigate the twists and turns of a long career, whereas employers won't.

This strategy is also very useful on job search and career groups.

Other Ways to Leverage Your Connections

When you find an online job posting that seems like a good fit, you are usually faced with uploading your resume into a corporate or headhunter database . . . and then waiting and waiting for a response. However, your social networks can quite possibly deliver direct contact with the people who can hire you or the people who know the people who can hire you. On all of your social networking sites, you can find people who work at your "companies of interest" or have done so in the past. Search for them, using the company name in your keyword search, then look for job titles one, two, and three levels above your own; for titles at your rank and one or two levels below it; and for job titles that interact with yours on a regular basis.

Once you have identified profiles of desirable titleholders, you can approach them to connect. You can do this based on your common professional interests or shared group membership, or with an e-mail stating your professional interests and attaching a resume. Check out *Knock 'em Dead Job Search Letter Templates* for sample social networking letters.

Other LinkedIn Resources

LinkedIn, like most social networking sites, offers an array of tools for your professional networking activities:

- Job postings from employers and headhunters
- Reminders of when to nurture your relationships with a follow-up call or e-mail
- Thousands of special-interest groups
- Links to job sites
- Offline social events to network in person

LinkedIn Is Just the Start

LinkedIn is just one of hundreds of social networking sites, and you'll find that most follow the same general format and request the same topics of information. We will move on now to examine the other three major social networking sites: Google+, Facebook, and Twitter. Because much of the profile information you'll be requested to provide will mirror what you needed to create your LinkedIn profile, we will focus on the variations that make these other sites different.

CHAPTER 7

GOOGLE+

Though newer than LinkedIn, Facebook, and Twitter, by the time you read this, Google+ may exceed one billion users. It has a professional focus similar to LinkedIn, but combines it with many of Facebook's attractions. Google+ also makes it easy to locate and connect with relevant and high-value professionals you don't know without requiring an introduction.

If you have a free Gmail account, you automatically have a Google+ account—you just have to complete your profile and then become part of the Google+ networking community. We talk elsewhere about the importance of keeping a separate e-mail address for career management issues; it would only make sense to use a Gmail address for this purpose.

Your Google+ Profile

Many of the sections of your Google+ profile correspond to similar ones already discussed in the chapter on LinkedIn. This is why I recommended that you save the latest version of your LinkedIn profile in a Microsoft Word document: It is then easier to customize and later copy and paste into other social media profiles. However, your Google+ and other social media profiles should not be exact replicas of each other. Each social networking site has its own personality that you need to reflect in some way. Besides, it's boring to anyone who looks at more than one of your profiles, and the Google search engine algorithms don't give you points for exact duplication. In fact, some authorities claim you will be penalized; unfortunately, to stop people gaming their algorithms, Google won't be precise on this issue.

Optimizing Headshots

Google is interested in optimized images, and having an optimized headshot will automatically help your visibility in Google searches. This is one of the techniques referred to by the revered SEO expert Will Kenderline for learning "the Google rain dance."

This means that when you show up in a Google search, the result will be accompanied by your headshot, and the evidence is clear that search results rise higher in the rankings and get more click-throughs than other links on the same page that do not have headshots.

HEADSHOT OPTIMIZATION STEPS

Will Kenderline advises cropping your picture to 500px by 500px, and saving it as a jpeg image, naming your file in this format:

JobTitleNameSurnameCityStateYear.JPG

For example, Will's headshot jpeg is titled:

DigitalMarketingStrategyConsultantWilliamKenderdine PhiladelphiaPA2014.JPG

If you are worried about stalkers, he advises you to just include your state.

You can use an optimized and other headshots for social networking. There are more steps you can take to optimize images than we have the space to discuss, but this will get you started. If you have difficulties with these first steps or want to take the optimization of visual images farther, talk to Will Kenderline; you can find him on LinkedIn.

Name

Use the name people use to address you at work, which means dropping the middle names, initials, Jrs, Srs, and I, II, III, and IVs, all of which will make you less discoverable. Just write the name you use in conversation every day. For example, my name is Martin John Yate, but I don't use Martin John Yate or Martin J. Yate because I want to use the name that people know me by and the name that's easiest to remember. Consequently, I just use Martin Yate in all my Internet activities and on all my social media platforms; you should make a similar choice.

Other Names

Some of us have names that always get misspelled; for example, a quarter of the people who reach out to me call me Martin Yates, rather than Martin Yate; ten percent think I'm related to the Irish poet W.B. Yeats and call me Martin Yeats; some misspell Yate as Yeat; and a few people call me Marty. Google cleverly recognizes this reality with a feature that allows you to add all those middle names, initials, Jrs, Srs, and I, II, III, and IVs, as well as other variations and common misspellings of your name under this heading. Adding in all the weird variations of your name that people use will help Google associate you correctly with search requests that contain these name variations.

Occupation

This is one of the first categories you'll see, and what you put here will appear as your headline. What goes in here is also important to search engine optimization—it's what makes you discoverable. It should contain the same messaging as your LinkedIn headline, but take the time to reword it while keeping it consistent with keywords and phrases recruiters are most likely to use in looking for someone like you.

The same goes for the rest of your profile: You can use most of your LinkedIn profile, but do take the time to reword it; this avoids the duplication that search engines penalize and creates unique content, which increases your discoverability. At the same time, however, be careful to keep the same messaging so that you don't confuse or dilute your brand. This isn't difficult: Just make it close but not an exact copy.

Professional Experience

For consistent messaging, use exactly the same information you used on LinkedIn, but do a little rewording so that it doesn't read like a carbon copy.

Watch out for dates and employers. When moving between different social media profiles and your resume, the number of your jobs and their employment dates can easily get jumbled.

You must exercise extreme caution in ensuring that this does not happen, as it can get your candidacy dismissed from consideration immediately. As the number of your job search and career management documents increases, oversights become more common. Whenever you complete a new social media profile, cross-check it against all other existing profiles and your resume to ensure compatibility.

Education

Start with your highest level of education and work backward through degrees, and remember to include ongoing professional education and accreditations. Just as with LinkedIn, you can add in prep schools and high school to increase your visibility to others.

Work Phone

Don't use your employer's phone number; instead, use a number that you consistently answer—probably your cell phone.

Other Profiles

Link to your other social networking profiles if they can add fresh but complementary views of you that don't conflict with your central messaging. From a practical perspective, if you have created profiles on LinkedIn, Twitter, Facebook, and Google+ over a period of time, there *will* be inconsistencies. So review each new or updated profile against the others for consistency before you make it public.

"Contributor to" and "Links"

Offer links to any blogs or websites you have contributed to. This helps people learn more about your knowledge and professionalism, and also helps with Google Authorship, which rewards creation of original content with increased visibility in search rankings.

Other Personal Information

While we are dealing with these personal issues, let's look at some Google+ profile headings that you may want to take a miss on.

Home Phone

Google+ also asks for a work phone, and that one is probably sufficient. This is a special consideration for women, who are more likely than men to be harassed by stalkers. If you are working, do not use your employer's phone number, but rather your preferred contact number.

BIRTHDAY

This is no one's business unless you choose for it to be. When you are younger it can work against you (lacks experience/maturity) or for you (young, eager, cheap). As you get older, it works almost exclusively *against* you because of age and wage discrimination issues. I would advise against supplying the world with your birthdate, and I'd also caution you to check that you haven't unwittingly revealed it on other social media sites.

GENDER

This can help distinguish you from others with the same or a similar name, but since gender can usually be identified by your headshot (which you *must* have), I'd consider leaving this one blank. Whatever your gender, it should be irrelevant to any professional activities and can only be used against you.

PLACES LIVED

Largely irrelevant unless it speaks to your cultural diversity or the geographic target location of your search. The first entry here should reflect where you live now. It's a big plus in a global economy if you have lived overseas or read or speak a foreign language, so you might try something like: "Iran, fluent Farsi. Singapore, basic Mandarin." I'd also include this under the Bragging Rights heading as well; the repetition will help your discoverability when languages and cultural awareness are an issue, as is the case with professionals working on the international stage.

Relationship

Personally oriented subject headings in your profile like this one are Google's attempt to be both LinkedIn (professionally oriented) and Facebook (socially oriented) by giving you control of who sees what on your profile. Your relationship status is entirely personal. Don't fill this in, unless you know it to be important to your profession. For example, there is a known bias in the long-distance trucking industry in favor of married men and women, because of perceived stability issues and because husband and wife teams often work together on the rig. However, this example is the exception rather than the rule.

Theoretically, you are able to control who sees what by means of different *Circles* (more on these shortly). This supposedly means that you can have oh-so-PC posts for your professional contacts and something else entirely for the people who know you socially. However, you will forget; you will accidentally mix the *Circles* and that VP at your dream company will see something she shouldn't—it's Murphy's Law: Anything that can go wrong, will go wrong. Until you consider yourself a social networking wizard, I recommend keeping your personal friends and family completely separate, perhaps leaving them for Facebook—at least for the time being.

Most people are relatively new to social networking and mistakes are both easy to make and often difficult to recover from. Because you are primarily using Google+ as a professional networking tool, you should keep your tone and all content consistently professional throughout—at least until you have the time to get fully familiar with these dual capabilities of Google+.

Bragging Rights

Google has examples such as "Survived high school, have 3 kids, etc."—which seems more traditionally Facebook-centric and not particularly useful for achieving your professional goals. Instead, use verifiable professional achievements or skills related to professional achievement, such as "Top regional sales last three years out of five" or "Member of Mensa and appeared on Jeopardy." If you have interests that support your professionalism, use them. For example, games like chess speak to your analytical skills, while distance running, swimming, and riding indicate both health and your determination and resiliency.

Profile Discovery

When your profile is complete, leave it for twenty-four hours and then come back and read it with fresh eyes. You will almost certainly make some tweaks. Once everything is just as you want it, check it against your resume and other social media profiles to ensure compatibility. Once this is done, you can enable *Profile Discovery*, which makes your profile public. All social media sites are the same in this respect, so check this final step across all your social networking sites.

PROFILE CONTROL

Google+ allows you to control how others view your profile. At the top right of your profile is a box entitled "View profile as." Here you can take a name from one of your *Circles* (to be discussed shortly), check how your profile appears to people in that *Circle,* and make any edits you deem suitable for that audience.

YOUR GOOGLE ADDRESS/URL

You'll have the opportunity to create a Google+ URL address. Think of this as a digital street address for the Internet. URL stands for "Universal Resource Locator" and it is a string of words, letters, and sometimes numbers that help search engines guide people to your profile.

To create this URL, Google+ asks for your name or nickname, then your current Google+ ID. Rather than using your name or nickname, which only your familiars know, you should try something that speaks to your profession, captures the essence of your *professional brand*, and hopefully adds to your discoverability, like KillerSystemsAnalyst or TopAccountant. If these are gone (and they probably are), you can try adding your area code or zip code—TopAccountant516—or your town—TopAccountant Charleston. Variations like these may not mean much to someone outside your target market, but in an age when companies shy away from relocation and use zip codes and city names in their search qualifiers, this approach can help your discoverability and quickly deliver useful information to harried recruiters.

Using a profession-oriented vanity URL also serves you in another way: It succinctly introduces the professional you and, because it refers to a job rather than your name, it has the added benefit of helping to protect your identity.

Privacy Settings

Your Google+ account has the flexibility to allow you to create a profile, part of which is public to the world and part of which is tightly restricted to specific types of people.

To start with, keep everything on Google+ profession oriented; that way all your communications can be left public. To share more selectively, you can find instructions when you click on the *Privacy Settings* link as you set up your profile. Personally I found these instructions confusing and decided that if my activity on this site was professional in all respects, I wouldn't need to worry about them.

Announce Your Status

Once your profile is completed, you can announce your status to the world. You can say you are in transition, and in the word count allowable talk about what you can do rather than boring everyone to tears with a detailed description of your ideal job. You can also do this in the "About" section of your Google+ profile, or by posting regular announcements that you are in transition and looking for opportunities.

When you do this, do it with confidence, sharing your target job title and the skills you bring to the professional table, never as some sad sack on the verge of breakdown.

If you are employed, you don't need to announce that you are looking to make a change. Doing so could jeopardize your current employment, and not making the announcement won't stop a recruiter who likes your skills from making an approach.

Communities

Communities on Google+ are similar to the groups on LinkedIn. Find Google+ *Communities* from the drop-down menu on your Google+ homepage. Again like LinkedIn, there are communities for any topic you can imagine. When you identify and join interesting communities, you'll become an active part of the community and will need to employ exactly the same behaviors we discussed for getting the best out of LinkedIn groups.

Building Google+ Circles

LinkedIn has established *Groups* that you can join, whereas Google+ has *Communities* you can join and *Circles* you can create and populate with whomever you want. You can create as many *Circles* as you wish using your own criteria for defining who goes into which *Circle*. You can add both people you know and people you don't know to your *Circles*.

Google+ gives you control of your profile and who gets to see what. You can drag and drop your contacts into the different *Circles* that you create, and thereby keep your employers and professional peers completely separate.

These contact *Circles* can be potential employers, contacts at companies, or others who are helping you get a job. You can keep them in one group or separate them out and send them relevant updates on your current job search. Keeping high-value hiring titles separate is helpful in maintaining your professionalism and controlling what information recruiters and potential hiring managers see about you.

Locating Contacts for Specific *Circles*

Let's say you're an accountant looking to create a *Circle* for high-value contacts—those people with job titles that imply the authority to hire you or professional contact with those authorities. All you need to do is a search within the Google+ site using "google.com google" followed by your choice of keywords, for example:

google.com google Accounting Manager
google.com google Manager of Accounting
google.com google Director of Accounting
google.com google Accounting Director
google.com google Finance Director
google.com google Director of Finance
google.com google Controller
google.com google V.P. of Finance
google.com google VP of Finance
google.com google Accountant
google.com google Purchasing

Repeating "google.com google" in your search term may seem strange, but it's just the way to get the Google+ search engine to find what you want efficiently.

Once a search delivers results, you decide who to put in each *Circle*. For example, it would make sense to put all those contacts with titles one or more levels above your own into their own *Circle* so that you can customize your messages to be of interest to that level of employer. Keeping employers away from professional colleagues is a good idea in a job search, because mingling the two could reveal potential competitors to recruiters.

When you post anything to your Google+ account, you can choose which *Circle* or *Circles* will see that post, photo, or video.

You can add contacts to your *Circles* without their authorization (as on LinkedIn) and/or with a request that they "friend" you back (as on Facebook).

Follow High-Level Contacts

As you find the names that go with your targeted high-value job titles and add them to a *Circle*, you are getting that much closer to *getting into conversations with the people in a position to hire you*. So when you ID an especially interesting prospect, follow his posts and, as appropriate opportunities arise, comment on them, or repost with the person's name and a flattering comment. Most people remember flattering comments, especially when reminded of them. Consequently, when you reach out to this person for direct communication, you can make reference to the post you commented on as an icebreaker.

You have the ability to assign different headshots for each of your *Circles*. However, I would recommend that at first you just use one great professional headshot for all your *Circles*, and then add additional *professional* headshots as you create them.

Other Unique Google+ Features

Streams, *Sparks*, and *Posts*

Streams keep you informed about what other people of interest are saying. They enable you to track information of interest both to you and to members of your *Circles*. *Posts* help you share your *Sparks* findings and your own original comments with individuals, *Circles*, and the world of people who might be interested in the same topics.

Streams

On your homepage you'll see your *Home Stream*. This tool collects and filters all the posts made by all the people in your different *Circles*. With the *All* filter selected, you can choose to see all these posts in either one long stream or by individual *Circle*: Choose to see results by *Circles*, because this gives you a greater ability to monitor and respond to items of interest. When you are engaged in a job search, reviewing the posts made by *Circles* that include recruiters and potential hiring managers should be a top priority, because these are posts that you can like or comment on, potentially building bridges of connection with the very people who can most influence your professional future.

Sparks

The *Sparks* function allows you to track posts, videos, and other information on topics of interest. This can contribute to your ongoing education and/or alert you to valuable information, which you can subsequently share with your *Circles*, identifying you as a committed and engaged professional who contributes to the common good.

On your homepage you can find *Sparks* underneath *Circles* near the top of the page. Google+ has set up a number of *Sparks* categories from which you can choose. Alternatively, you can type a keyword or phrase into the search box and view the results.

When you like the results that come from either of these options, click *Add* (underneath the search box). *Sparks* maintains a steady stream of interesting and professionally relevant information for you and to share with your *Circles*. To share with your *Circles*, just click the *Share* button that appears under every result.

Now while *Sparks* will help you generate an ongoing flow of relevant information to share and increase your visibility and enhance the value of your brand, you can also use it to gather insights into any company with whom you've landed an interview. Along with *Sparks*, you can also use Google Reader, Google News, Google Media, and Google Alerts.

Posts

You can choose to share any posts you make with particular *Circles*, or you can post publicly. If you choose to post publicly, people who have added you to their *Circles* will see your posts. Making your posts public allows Google+ to index your expertise and supply it as a link in response to other people's queries on this topic, which makes you and your knowledge discoverable by a much wider audience. Just be aware, though, that if you post something and it's re-shared, your friends in that *Circle* will be able to see the post even if the original post was not shared with them. You can avoid this when you click the down arrow button in your post and choose "disable re-share."

You also have the option of editing your posts once they are published, which is not an option with LinkedIn unless you do it within a few seconds. Nevertheless, as a matter of habit, I strongly recommend that any post you make is first written and spell-checked in a Word document.

You increase credibility and visibility and enhance your brand when you ask interesting questions and share interesting information with the people in your *Circles*. *Streams* and *Sparks* will help you filter information flow so that you only post relevant insights from reliable third-party resources. Whatever you post should be of immediately recognizable value to the audience you have created with a particular *Circle*. You can include comments and/or pictures to enhance what you find interesting.

Google+ Hangouts

The future is here. Hangouts are Google+'s version of group video chat (like Skype), and allow you to join in conversations with people in your field. These video chats are currently limited to ten people; however, they can broadcast to an unlimited number, so I can see it being used as a platform for industry experts to share their expertise with much larger audiences. Look for *Knock 'em Dead Hangouts* coming soon!

You can also expect this tool to be used by headhunters, corporate recruiters, and hiring managers for remote interviews. When you have long-distance video interviews coming up, be sure to read Chapter 15 for tips on how to ace these awkward events.

Google+ is a financial powerhouse with every intention of dominating the social networking scene, so you can expect ongoing enhancements to the networking capabilities of Google+. For now, you have plenty of information to start leveraging the unique possibilities of Google+. Next we'll look at Facebook.

CHAPTER 8

FACEBOOK

Facebook is the epitome of social networking, insomuch as the majority of its many millions of users use it as a social and at times intensely personal communication platform: "Great party last night, booyah!", "My girlfriend dumped me," "Look at this weird thing I'm eating," and "I wuv you Pookie," to cite just a few examples I've seen.

For reasons like these, many people are leery of using Facebook as a serious professional networking platform. However, if you do—and as we'll see, there are some very good reasons why you should use Facebook as part of your social networking program—you have to keep your profile professional in word and tone.

Your Facebook Profile

Many of the sections of your Facebook profile correspond to similar ones already discussed in the previous chapters on LinkedIn and Google+, so you should be getting a general idea of what belongs here and what doesn't. Accordingly, we'll focus on those portions of the Facebook profile that differ in some way from social networking sites we have already discussed.

On Facebook your profile appears under the heading *Timeline*. While it allows you to include all the professional information you'd expect on LinkedIn or Google+, Facebook focuses on your personal life by encouraging casual photos (which you should approach with professional caution), showing your recent activities (keep them professional), whom you recently connected with (like the other sites), who and what you have recently *liked*, what you've been watching on Netflix or Hulu, and the music you've been listening to on Spotify. Like LinkedIn, you can show covers of books you've recently read (a good advertisement opportunity for your dedication to professional matters).

Now you can hide or highlight these and many more features, but talking about and sharing your tastes and the most personal information about yourself is strangely addictive. While writing this chapter, I was checking my page and got sucked into all kinds of fun daydreams about music, movies, and vacations, which from a professional networking perspective are time-wasting activities and if published indiscriminately showcase the "personal me" rather than my *professional persona* and brand.

To help you keep yourself focused on the *professional brand* you want to promote, keep this thought in mind: You are trying to get hired, not dated. There's an app we'll discuss in a couple of paragraphs that will help you keep things professional.

An app called Bright (*www.bright.com*) allows you to import your profile from LinkedIn, which will make your setup that much easier. Just remember to alter it slightly to maintain readers' attention and get yourself discovered by search engine algorithms.

Hometown

You probably filled in your hometown, but this can be open to misinterpretation. Some people consider "hometown" to be where they live now, others where they were born and spent their early years. Recruiters search by skills and by geographic location (to avoid relocation costs), so you might consider entering the name of your current city of residence. In an age in which relocation is seen as a barrier to recruitment, I have known professionals in transition who are intent on moving from say, Phoenix to Nashville, to list Nashville as their current residence in order to overcome that barrier. I'm not recommending this, but people are doing it.

Clean Up Your Profile

You need to maintain a consistently professional message across all your chosen networking sites, because recruiters can and do search across all these social media platforms, not only to find initial candidates, but to help winnow candidates throughout the selection cycle.

If you grew up with social networking, there are probably details of your wilder times available online for the world to see. You need to do searches for yourself to discover exactly what is out there about you. When you find something that is inappropriate for your professional image, go back and clean up your digital dirt.

I just returned from an appearance at a major convention for college career services and corporate campus recruiters. It was noted at the conference that upward of 80 percent of recruiters are using publicly available online data about short-list candidates as a screening tool. Twenty-five percent said they would reject a candidate based on this information. This means we all have to police the image we have online, so delete those once-amusing pictures of you projectile vomiting at a frat party. As an example of how bad the repercussions can get from just photographs, in December 2013 the *Huffington Post* reported on a man who was indicted for 143 felony counts, based on evidence gathered from his Instagram photos—ouch.

Your mantra needs to be: cause the least offense to the greatest majority of people. For professional networking purposes, you should leave out references to sexual, political, or religious issues, because whatever your POV is, it is guaranteed to cause offense to someone who might otherwise offer you a great professional opportunity. Your profile can still represent the real you without causing offense in these areas. There's a neat app called Reppler that will review your profiles, help you manage your online image across all social networks, and alert you to questionable content.

Privacy Settings

If you are determined to include content that common sense or Reppler finds questionable, make sure that your privacy settings are very strict. Set them to just *friends*; even *friends of friends* leaves you open to danger. With the *friends only* setting, employers won't be able to see the details of your profile, your photos, or your personal status updates.

Restricting Access

On your Account page, choose *Edit Friends* from the dropdown menu, then *Create List*. For employers and recruiters, you can create a *High-Value Titles* or *Restricted* list and add them to that, rather like the way we discussed putting all your high-value management connections into their own *Circle* on Google+. Make sure that this *Circle* (on Facebook, your *High-Value Titles* or *Restricted* list) receives only audience-appropriate posts from you. People on this list will only see posts you tag as "public."

Also, if you have connections with crazies who have no concern for their professional reputation or who post sexual, religious, or political comments, or comments about employers or coworkers, you can deactivate your "wall" until you land that new job. Alternatively, you could quietly de-friend them until the transition is completed. Whether or not it's fair, the reality is that you are judged by the behavior of the company you keep. People have been terminated for inappropriate comments about employers and coworkers, and you could be deemed guilty by association.

Becoming Discoverable

Facebook is one of the biggest websites in the world, and your profile is one of hundreds of millions. In effect, you are a single indistinguishable stalk of wheat in the vast prairie lands of America. This means that unless someone is looking for you in particular, recruiters' searches for your professional skill set will only find you when you do everything you can to make yourself discoverable with the profile you create and by the activities you engage in on Facebook.

First off, your Facebook profile, along with your posts (clean up any questionable past comments), need to complement the messaging you have on LinkedIn, Google+, and any other social networking sites. While the information you share and how you share it can vary, the messages you send and comment on should be compatible with your established *professional brand* and the messaging you use on all your social media sites.

"Liking" and "Following" Company Pages
About 80 percent of American companies, beyond local mom and pop operations, have a social media presence on one or more

of the big four social recruiting sites, and while eight out of ten use social media to recruit, a recent study of corporate recruiters found that 87 percent of them said that the best way to get on company radar is to "like" the company's page.

If you take the time to identify desirable employers in your target job search area (I'll show you how to do this later in the book), you can then visit each of your social networking sites, search for that company's homepage, and "follow" them. If you choose to follow that company's page, their posts will show up in your *newsfeed* under their *list* heading.

This allows you to become much more visible to that company's recruiters by responding to comments and posting questions (non-self-serving) of your own. When company recruiters make posts, add a "like" to the post and, when appropriate, make an intelligent comment or ask a question; this will increase your visibility. Because social media is still new as a recruiting tool, recruiters are excited about it and want success stories, so they pay attention to their social media company pages—and that certainly can't hurt your candidacy. Any "games" you find on a company page are quite likely to be tied to skills and aptitude in some way, so if you play them, expect your involvement to be part of the recruitment process: Don't leave anything unfinished, and "play" like the serious professional you are. An interesting approach I've heard to gaming these disguised aptitude tests is to have a friend who would never be interested in this company permit you to log under his name, allowing you to preview the test. Sneaky, I know, but isn't the company being equally sneaky by not being upfront about their intent?

When an interesting position is posted, post a wall comment stating that you carry a similar job title and asking whom you can approach with questions. Once you have a name and means of direct communication, you are getting very close to . . . you got it: *getting into conversation with someone in the recruitment and selection cycle.*

Facebook Communities

For like-minded people who may not initially know each other, LinkedIn has *Groups*, Facebook has *Communities*, and Google+ has *Circles* and *Communities*. These pages all work in similar ways and offer similar benefits. You add value to a *Group* when you "like" existing discussions, comment on them positively, or start your own discussions. When you do this, you also become more visible, and if your comments/discussions are carefully thought out, they can impress recruiters and professional colleagues. You can also find alumni groups and job search groups, just like on LinkedIn.

Find Conferences

Many online and offline conferences also set up Facebook pages for event promotion. These pages can be useful, giving you access to people involved in the conference. Search by "conference," "webinar," and "teleconference" plus variations based on your areas of interest.

Build Your Network

Just because Facebook has more of a frat-house reputation than, say, LinkedIn or Google+, that doesn't mean you should skip searching for and connecting with the high-value titles for your job search in just the same way you would on other sites through communities, groups, conferences, etc.

The bigger your network, the more likely you are to have an inside connection at companies you'd like to approach. Look for friends and colleagues, coworkers, former managers, college friends, and so on. Re-establishing connections with people you've known allows you to ask what they are doing and share news about your life. These contacts will in turn bring you within reach of new potential connections.

Think International

While high-value contacts in the target area of your job search are obviously the most valuable, Facebook has more international members than any other networking site, so it is worth looking out for overseas connections. With the huge number of multinational corporations in existence today, this may or may not help you in a job search today, but your social networks should be a long-term career management tool, and you never know what twists and turns your career will take over the years, or when knowing someone in Mumbai could deliver just the lead you need. You can duplicate these searches on both LinkedIn and Google+.

Connect with Recruiters and Headhunters

Recruiters live on social media sites, so you can find headhunters and corporate recruiters who live in your area and add them as friends. With a *friend request*, always add a personal note explaining why you want to add them as a friend. Headhunters' and recruiters' lifeblood is connectivity, so most will accept, and with that connection you have just gotten that much closer to starting a conversation that could lead to interviews and job offers—so much smarter than loading your resume in databases and waiting for calls to come in.

Status Updates

With social networking, being helpful and paying it forward is important. Read your connections' updates regularly, "like" them, and whenever you can offer help, do so.

If you are in a job search, you should also add two or three search-related posts each week, generated from the resources we discussed earlier. Give an update on your current situation in one of them, and make the other two offers of help; a good idea is to post about jobs you've stumbled across that aren't a fit for you, for example: "As you know, I'm looking for a new accounting opportunity, and last night I came across an Accounting Manager's job at a blue chip company. It's not for me, but if you know anyone who's looking, I'd be glad to pass on some info." This way you are seen as a supportive member of your professional community, and this will increase your credibility and visibility, not to mention your connection count; and by sharing job postings you will automatically attract new high-value connections.

Two or three job search–related updates a week might seem like overkill, but people are forgetful, and while you might write three status updates, that doesn't mean all your contacts read or see any of them. By updating your network with your job search updates, you stay in the forefront of their minds. Hootsuite saves you time and enables you to manage your social networks by posting comments across all your social networking sites at once.

Useful Facebook Job Search Apps

By the time you read this, Facebook could have more than 3 million jobs posted, and there are a growing number of apps that can be useful in your job search. For example:

Graph Search

When you see an interesting opportunity, you can flag it and use Graph Search to find connections. For example, if you see a job with Bloomberg Media, you can ask it to search for "Bloomberg" and it will search all your connections that mention the search word or phrase. You can also use Graph Search to find Facebook members who work at that company and view their public information (such as groups they are involved with), which can open the door to conversation and connection. This app also allows you to find companies and analyze the personal interests of its employees.

SimplyHired

SimplyHired is a job aggregator that cruises around 4,000 sites on your behalf. The neat wrinkle here is that when you sign in with your Facebook account, you can see jobs available at your friends' employers.

Branchout

Branchout, Facebook's app for professional networking, is designed to help you leverage your social networks for job search and professional development, and it's quite impressive. It currently has over 800 million professional profiles, and it's growing every day. It's the largest networking service on Facebook. You can use it in a couple of valuable ways:

- To search for job postings
- To search for connections at these companies

When you create a brief professional profile on Branchout, you become visible to the hordes of recruiters who search this enormous database every day. Branchout, though a Facebook property, is a separate website, with its focus on professional networking, so your behavior in all matters (profile creation, headlines, introductions, endorsements) should follow the protocols you live by when on LinkedIn or Google+.

Cachinko

Cachinko is another job aggregator that searches other sites for jobs meeting your needs. It also lets you refine your search by giving it feedback on why a particular job was a good or bad fit.

Bright

Bright lets you search for jobs on CareerBuilder. It can also tell you where friends in your network are working. It allows you to identify network connections that work at companies of interest to you. As mentioned at the beginning of the chapter, this app also lets you import your profile from LinkedIn, making your Facebook setup a lot faster.

IntheDoor

IntheDoor allows you to see where the contacts in your network are working and the jobs available at those companies.

Inside Job

Inside Job helps you search for jobs, and will identify others who also use Inside Job and who work at companies you have identified as desirable.

Facebook Marketplace

Facebook Marketplace, apart from helping you buy stuff from other Facebook users, can help you find jobs by setting up automated searches with results sent to your e-mail.

Social Jobs

Social Jobs connects you to open positions where you live.

Facebook in Your Networking Strategy

I don't think Facebook is going to surpass LinkedIn as the number one professional networking site just yet. However, it is becoming more useful every day and should definitely be part of your networking plan of attack. With the tactics we've discussed and the growing list of tools built for the site, the odds of Facebook adding real value to your search are now steadily improving. Just remember that Facebook really is geared to the social side of life, and while it is developing assets focused on the professional side, you still have to be careful not to be wooed into making inappropriate comments.

CHAPTER 9

TWITTER

"Tweeting" is Twitter slang for making a post. Twitter allows a user to make tweets of 140 characters; including spaces and a hyperlink, that's about one short sentence. You can't say much of weight in 140 characters.

For this and other reasons, when Twitter first launched, it wasn't immediately clear how the service could be used effectively by job hunters or professionals looking for new career management tools. Gradually, though, useful applications evolved, and now the service has a real role in both job search and career management.

Twitter is useful in a job search for tracking companies, recruiters, headhunters, and the activities of high-value job titles in your profession. You can, of course, also tweet to your heart's content, but using Twitter to *listen* to what your professional world is doing will lead you to companies, jobs, and recruiters of interest. Once you have created a profile and begun to identify the companies and high-value people you want to become visible to, intelligent tweeting activities can put you on the radar of high-value contacts in a way that showcases your *professional persona* as thoroughly engaged and committed.

Twitter Is Better for Some Jobs Than Others

Twitter is best for finding certain kinds of jobs. Tom Gimbel, CEO of LaSalle Network, said on *CBS Moneywatch* in 2013 that "the positions for which Twitter is most relevant in the hiring process are entry- to mid-level positions that are remote, both nationally and globally; in e-commerce; brand managers of marketing; computer coders; data architects; and so forth. Where it's not so prevalent is in the mainstream positions, including sales, accounting, finance, call center representatives, and human resources."

However, corporate usage is growing rapidly, and as each month passes, more and more mainstream employers are becoming involved with Twitter. This means that more mainstream jobs are being promoted from this platform.

This trend will continue to gather momentum. Don't discount Twitter's relevance to your job search until you have read and tried the tactics in this section. You might be pleasantly surprised.

Your Twitter Profile

Many of the sections required for your Twitter profile correspond to the components we discussed in your other social media profiles. You should be getting an idea of how these profiles work, so in our discussion of Twitter, we'll just look at those parts of the profile where Twitter adds new twists to the conversation.

Twitter Handle

When you sign up for Twitter, you have to select a "Twitter handle," which is the name you become known by when you tweet (express your own thoughts) or retweet (share the thoughts and information of others). The same considerations apply here as applied to your headline on LinkedIn; your presence is profession oriented, so your handle should speak to your job and your profession in some way. Checking out the Twitter handles of other people in your profession can also give you ideas for handles that support rather than hurt your brand.

Professional Headshot

You should always have a headshot on your social media profiles. Google tells us that, given a page of links, the ones with headshots will always be viewed first. This makes the effort of generating a professional-looking headshot worth the effort and expense. On Twitter, people are likely to visit your profile in response to your tweets and retweets, and your headshot is the first thing they will see. Optimizing your headshot images, as we discussed in Chapter 6, will help increase your discoverability.

Bio

Coming right after your headshot will be your bio/profile. This should state your job title and capture the essence of your responsibilities and your work capabilities, and do so in an informal, "cut-to-the-chase" manner reflective of the Twitter approach to communication. If you accept the commonsense approach of the *Knock 'em Dead* career management philosophy, you will have completed a Target Job Deconstruction on your target job (as we discussed in Chapter 5) as the first step in creating social media profiles that speak with a consistent voice about your *professional persona*. Read a few Twitter profiles and then, using the TJD information that is most important in capturing your professional skills and abilities, edit it to match Twitter's informal style to the extent you can without sounding unprofessional.

ANNOUNCE YOUR AVAILABILITY

It is perfectly acceptable to announce that you are in transition and looking for new opportunities. Mostly this will be seen by the people with whom you have established connections, but with the right hashtags you will get the attention of a wider audience that was not previously familiar with you.

Hashtags

The big problem with all social media is filtering out the white noise of irrelevant information. *Hashtags*—searchable terms used in tweets and identified by a preceding pound sign, for example: #job search, #accountantjobs—help the Twitter search engine categorize and find messages that follow a common theme.

You can use hashtag terms to find job opportunities and profession-relevant information. You can also use them in your tweets to share information with your own Twitter contacts (followers), as well as to attract new followers who have similar interests.

They can help build your Twitter network with a relevant and distinct focus. You can use them anywhere in a tweet: at the beginning, middle, or end.

You can increase your visibility with recruiters who are looking for people like you with hashtags like:

- **#resume.** Be sure to give a link to your resume on LinkedIn or another networking site where you have loaded it, thereby ensuring wider exposure for your resume and the deeper details of your social media profile.
- **#profile, #LinkedIn, #Google+, #Facebook.** Whenever you are tweeting about your skills, these hashtags will alert readers to your profile on these social networking sites.

- **#accountant.** (Or whatever your job title may be.) Recruiters will look for people by their job title, and using an appropriate hashtag helps them find you.
- # **"A key skill."** If you possess an in-demand skill, recruiters will be using that as a search term. Placing a hashtag in front of that word or phrase makes it, and you, more discoverable, for example: #MBA, #Leanmanagement, #datasourcing.

Some people recommend hashtags like #unemployed or #needajob, but I feel that these make you sound altogether hopeless. They're the online version of that poor homeless person's sign reading: "Will work for food."

Twitter Job Leads

Companies and headhunters use Twitter to share good news about their activities and to post jobs because it is a fast, cheap, and effective way to get the word out. *You* will use it to:

- Learn about job opportunities
- Share the ones that aren't right for you as you retweet and mention them in your other social networking activities
- Retweet the company's more interesting announcements

Because social networking is new *and* makes the recruitment process easier, corporate recruiters and headhunters watch these channels carefully and pay attention to those professionals smart enough to get on their radar.

If you use the direct research and approach tactics I address in Chapter 14, by the time you start using Twitter you will have identified every company of interest and every headhunter who works within the target location of your job search. You can then find and follow them on Twitter. Once identified, you can get their tweets linked to your Twitter feed, so that their tweets come to you automatically for review at your convenience—which makes for efficient use of your time.

My friend the social networking expert Josh Waldman has an excellent YouTube video called *Use Twitter as a Job Board* that discusses some of these issues in more detail.

How to Become Visible to Recruiters

Recruiters tweet about specific job openings and share information about the employer—and to a lesser degree, general information of interest to their target audience. Following a company on Twitter also gives you insight into their activities and their culture, and these insights can help you tailor your communications with that company.

Recruiters will notice that you are a follower and that you "like" and retweet their posts. This will lead them to look at your tweets and profile; in other words, it increases your visibility.

By following companies and individual recruiters, you will hear about job openings, and when they aren't relevant to your needs but might be helpful to your network, you should retweet them (as you should a recruiter's other profession-related tweets). This will raise your visibility with the company recruiters.

Some of the common hashtags used by employers to make their employment needs more discoverable include:

#hiring
#joblisting
#jobopening
#jobpostings
#employment
#opportunity

You can use these hashtags as search terms, both on their own and followed by a job title and/or key skills.

Good Twitter Apps for Job Tracking

Apps that help you discover and track jobs can obviously be a great timesaver. You should check out:

Jobs at Twitter
Twitjobs
TweetMyJobs
JobShouts
MicroJobs
NearbyTweets

All of these apps find jobs close to your stated current address. Each of these apps has a slightly different angle of attack, so all six are worth checking out.

You Are What You Tweet

Next to informing you about job opportunities, your Twitter presence is best suited to help increase your visibility and credibility by allowing you to share professionally relevant information and resources with a wider audience. To become a source of interest to others who don't know you personally, the focus of your tweets has to be professional and relevant.

What you tweet and who you quote create an indelible impression about who you are. Apart from the previously mentioned sources of prevetted information, you should check out SmartBrief, where you can sign up for any of hundreds of free newsletters that feed you a stream of information of potential interest to your audience.

You can tweet fifty times a day if you want, but tweeting takes time, and many recruiters and others in your profession will wonder what you are doing for a living, or for your job search, if you spend all day tweeting.

Increase Ur Tweet Content

Twitter only allows tweets of 140 characters *including a link*, and this limitation requires you to be concise in everything you say. As the purpose of any tweet is to drive the reader to more detailed information, try to think of your tweets as headlines. Many Twitter users feel that posting a headline as a question draws people to click on your link and answer your question. I'm writing this in December and my wife Angela and I recently tweeted "Unemployed? Here are Six Free Holiday Gifts to Give Yourself," followed by a compressed link to a blog that we'd written and posted on the *Knock 'em Dead* website about being good to yourself when times are tough and the holidays are coming. We asked a question, teased an answer, and supplied a hyperlink in fewer than 100 characters, spaces included.

Your tweets need to demonstrate that you have strong *written communication skills* for the medium. Writing for Twitter has rules that are different from traditional communication, so when you can't get your tweet and hyperlink into the allowed 140 characters including spaces, you'll need to start abbreviating. Here are some of the abbreviations you can use in tweets:

- AB/ABT – About
- AFAIK – As far as I know
- B4 – Before
- BGD – Background
- BTW – By the way
- CHK – Check
- DYK – Did you know/Do you know

- EM/EML – E-mail
- EMA – E-mail address
- FB – Facebook
- FOTD – Find of the day
- HTH – Happy to help
- HOTD – Headline of the day
- HT – Heard through
- ICYMI – In case you missed it
- IDK – I don't know
- IIRC – If I remember correctly
- IMHO – In my humble opinion
- OH – Overheard
- PLMK – Please let me know
- SM – Social media
- SN – Social network
- QOTD – Quote of the day
- TFTF – Thanks for the follow
- TFTT – Thanks for this tweet
- TY – Thank you
- TYIA – Thank you in advance
- TYVM – Thank you very much
- YT – YouTube

There are many more accepted Twitter abbreviations; just Google for them.

How to Compress Long Hyperlinks

As you know, links can be very long, and your 140 character–limited tweets must also include the link you want readers to follow for more detailed information. Fortunately, there are tools that compress your links called URL shorteners. The one I have always used is Bitly, which can shorten a long URL to just a few characters. You just copy the original link into a dialogue box, and within seconds Bitly delivers a compressed version comprising just a few characters.

Think Before You Tweet

All professional jobs require good judgment and a positive attitude, so keep your tweets free of negativity, questionable comments, and absolutely stay away from politics or religion because, whatever your beliefs on these issues, you are guaranteed to annoy at least 50 percent of your audience—the very people who could have your next job within their grasp.

Think about all the celebrities (not to mention private individuals) who have gotten into hot water because of a thoughtless tweet. It's very easy to forget that what you say on Twitter—and on social media sites generally—is going out for the world to see and can never be retracted.

Sources for Tweets and Retweets

Following experts prominent in your profession gives you content to retweet that adds to your credibility and puts you in good company. By consistently sharing intelligent commentary on your profession and its issues, you might not become an overnight industry expert, but you will be taken that much more seriously by those who could hire you. Here are some good sites for finding these experts:

- Twellow is a very useful search directory searchable by area of expertise, profession, and other attributes listed in people's personal profiles on Twitter—which means you can find someone by employer and then filter by using your high-value job titles.
- wthashtag.com and wefollow.com identify influential tweeters in your profession and industry.

- MuckRack, Twiangulate, and FollowerWonk identify influential tweeters, but not necessarily by profession.

You Are Who You Retweet

The Internet has given us a world in which anyone can state that they are the world's greatest authority on everything, but that doesn't necessarily make it so. Verify the credentials of the people you listen to and subsequently quote in your tweets and posts on other social networking sites, because to people you don't know, you are who you quote.

Distraction: The Biggest Problem of Networking

The biggest problem you face with social networking today is not lack of social networking sites, but too much aimless socializing. The times when you are networking to find a job tend to be moments of uncertainty, and this causes a degree of insecurity for anyone.

At times like these, friendly comments and faux compliments (nowhere worse than on Twitter) can act like addictive drugs to our fragile egos, with the need for affirmation overtaking the need to *get into conversation with the people who can hire you*. This presents a danger of getting too involved with social networking activities that lack clear goals, which is why we'll shortly begin to talk about integrating networking into every aspect of your job search.

We have talked about LinkedIn, Google+, Facebook, and Twitter, and there are many more networking sites that could be useful for your job search. However, you should be careful to focus your energies on a handful of sites, rather than dilute the impact of your social networking activities with a minimal presence on too many. Add a presence on other social networking sites once you are fully familiar with how to leverage the benefits of the major sites in your job search.

Any successful professional networking strategy also leverages a handful of additional online and offline networks too, and these are what we will turn to next.

CHAPTER 10

PROFESSIONAL AND
ALUMNI NETWORKS

Professional Associations

One of the best things you can do for a job search or your long-term career success is to develop a relationship with your professional community with membership in a professional association. Not only will you gain from the online events, blogs, discussions, and ongoing professional education at the association's website, but by attending the association's regular offline meetings of your local chapter, you will get to know, and be known by, the best-connected and most professionally committed professionals in your area—literally the inner circle of your profession.

Know and Be Known

Professional associations have monthly meetings in all major metropolitan areas, plus regional and national get-togethers every year. Unless you work on a national level, membership in the local or state chapters of a national association will be quite sufficient for your needs—and cheaper, too. Membership will help you stay attuned to the ways technology and a global economy are constantly changing the way you work, and the regular training programs will increase your skills and knowledge, helping you stay current with new skills. These activities combine to make your current job more secure, and to make you a more desirable candidate for better jobs with your current employer or with a new one.

The professional association is a new "old boy" network for the modern world. Your membership is a link to millions of colleagues throughout your profession, the vast majority of whom will gladly talk to you based on your connection through the association. If you are a member of a local chapter, you often won't have access to members of other chapters, but with social networking on LinkedIn, Google+, Facebook, and Twitter you'll be able to find association members around the country with relative ease.

All industries and professions have multiple associations, any one of which could be valuable depending on your needs. For example, if you are in retail, you can join any of some thirty national associations and fifty state associations. Together these associations represent employees of more than 1.5 million retail organizations, which in turn provide employment for more than 18 million people. Most other associations offer similarly impressive networking potential.

Minority Associations

If you fit the profile of a special-interest or identifiable minority group, you will also find professional associations that cater especially to you. These include—but are by no means limited to—associations for African Americans, Latinos, Asian Americans, professionals with disabilities, and women; another benefit is that companies actively recruit identifiable minorities.

How to Find Associations

When you join a professional association, it represents a new level of networking for you—face-to-face relations with high-value contacts who work in local companies that are probably employment options for you. A good place to start looking for the right association is online, with Wikipedia's professional associations page. In your local library, check out the *Encyclopedia of Associations* (published by Gale); you can gain digital access to this resource, but it isn't cheap, so I recommend you check to see if your library, university career services office, or alumni association has online access first.

Alternatively, you can execute a Google search for relevant keywords. For example, "legal association" will generate listings of associations for the legal profession. You should also search variations such as "law associations." If you belong to any identifiable minority, you might try a search such as "Asian legal association" or "women in law."

Professional Associations Need You

When you join an association, you'll benefit greatly from attending the offline meetings, because this is where you get to know the other players in your local professional community. Most local chapters have a monthly meeting that you should attend. But don't just passively attend meetings; get involved. At all but the national level, associations are exclusively volunteer organizations and always need someone to set out chairs or hand out paperwork and name tags. The task itself doesn't matter, but your visible willingness to be an active participant most certainly does, and it will get you on a first-name basis with people you would probably never meet otherwise.

Given the nature of association membership, you don't have to go straight from introductions to asking for leads on jobs. In fact, it can be productive to have initial conversations where you do not ask for leads or help in your job search, but where you make a contribution to the group. This is always preferable, because others are more likely to help you when they see you making an effort toward the common good.

Volunteer

Once you have the lay of the land, volunteer for one of the many committees that are needed to keep your chapter running. It's the best way to meet people and expand your sphere of influence, as you can reach out to others while you engage in your volunteer association activities. Associations invariably employ the "many hands make light work" approach. Committee involvement doesn't take much time, because committees are structured to function with the help of full-time professionals like you who have lives to live and many other responsibilities.

From a networking point of view, the bigger the committee, the better. Membership and program committees are among the best to join. However, involvement in any committee will serve your needs, because committee membership enables you to reach out to those on other committees. Conference and events committees are great to join, because not only are they always in need of willing hands, you can leverage membership on them to initiate contact with just about anyone in your professional world: "Hi, Bill Parsons? I'm Becky Lemon with the conference committee of the local association. I'd like to invite you to a meeting we are having next week on . . ."

If you volunteer and become active in an association, the people with whom you come in contact will begin to identify you as a *team player* and part of the profession's inner circle—and, as I have mentioned throughout the *Knock 'em Dead* series, the inner circle is where job security, special assignments, raises, and promotions live, not to mention ready referrals for open positions.

Association Databases and Directories

Access to the association database comes with your membership and delivers a superb networking resource for telephone and e-mail networking campaigns with fellow professionals who live in your own part of the country. You can feel comfortable calling any other member on the phone and introducing yourself: "Hi, Angela Ciccine? My name is Martin Yate. We haven't spoken before, but we are both members of the Social Media Management Association. I need some advice; can you spare a minute?"

Your mutual membership, and the commitment to your profession that it bespeaks, will guarantee you a few moments of anyone's time—a courtesy you should always return.

You can also use your association membership database/directory to generate personal introductions for jobs you have heard about elsewhere. For example, you might have found an interesting job posting on a company website with the request that you upload your resume; this is where your networking can pay big dividends.

Apply just as requested on the website where you found the job, then return to your membership database to find people who work for, or have worked for, that company. A judicious call or two will frequently get you a personal referral: You have just *doubled your chances of landing that interview.*

These same contacts can help you prepare for the interview with insider knowledge about the company, the department, and the hiring manager. In Chapter 17, we will discuss how to *more* than double your chances of landing interviews with more social network–integrated job search tactics that can *triple* and *quadruple* your odds of success.

Association Job Postings

Companies post job openings with professional associations because they know the applicants will be qualified. For this reason, you will often see job postings on the website that sometimes don't appear anywhere else. In down economic times, a savvy corporate recruiter will use an association website to skim the cream of available talent while at the same time screening out the less committed.

Newsletters and Blogs

Professional associations all have online blogs and e-mail–delivered newsletters. You'll notice that association members write almost all of the blogs and the articles in the newsletters. Everyone likes to have his literary efforts appreciated, and telling a member you have read an article he's written gives you a great introduction to a networking call.

Such active social networking with the association's membership puts you on the radar of all the best-qualified and best-connected professionals in your area.

Associations, Social Media Profiles, and Resumes

List professional associations on all your social media profiles and at the end of your resume under a "Professional Affiliations" heading. This is guaranteed to get a second glance, as it signifies professional awareness. Recruiters belong to the associations that represent their recruiting interests and will use association names in their database searches, so association membership will also help both your social media profiles and your resume achieve greater discoverability.

Alumni Associations

Every school, from Acme Welding to Harvard Law, has an alumni association, and being a member can play a pivotal role in your professional life. Historically, alumni associations have existed to raise money from alumni for the school, but in these uncertain economic times, alumni associations increasingly see career outreach as a cost-efficient way to stay in touch with alumni.

If you are an alumni member, you have access to the alumni association membership database, which puts you in touch with other graduates. People like to extend their help to those with whom they share a college experience.

Additionally, going to the meetings and occasionally volunteering for an alumni project are activities that will ease you into collegial relationships with men and women on every rung of the corporate ladder—people who are in a position to boost your career.

Alumni associations all have online blogs and newsletters, and most now include job postings. An increasing number even have semiformalized job-hunting networks in which alumni are encouraged to share employment needs.

Building an Alumni Database

Your alumni association is a valuable network just waiting for you to connect and leverage your contacts intelligently. You can look for alumni who hold any of the high-value job titles in the target location of your job search, and whenever you upload your resume in response to a job posting, also cross-check your alumni database for people who have worked for that company. Look first for members who hold a job title one to three levels above your own, and then for any of the other high-value job titles. Using the same approach we discussed with professional association contacts, *you can again double your chances of that job posting turning into an interview.*

If you don't know the URL of your alma mater, go to *www .utexas.edu/world/univ/.* For community college URLs, you'll find an excellent resource at *www.mcli.dist.maricopa.edu/.* Another site with job search relevance is *www.classmates.com.*

Company Alumni Associations

In recent years larger, more widely dispersed companies have seen increased value in maintaining contact with ex-employees, since these people provide a source for future hires or leads on future hires. Corporate HR departments are doing this through online corporate alumni associations, sometimes freestanding, sometimes as a group on LinkedIn. Go to:

- JobHunt.org for a comprehensive list of corporate alumni associations
- Alumni.net for a list of company, university, high school, and other alumni associations and their members all over the world

As I write this, I am in the smallish town of Savannah, Georgia, and as soon as the Alumni.net page loaded it told me of 10,688 jobs in Savannah and 208,000 in Georgia.

Your Past Managers and Other References as a Networking Resource

It is a major mistake not to speak at all to the people you will need to use as references, or only to speak to them at the end of your search, when a job offer is imminent. While as a rule we are confident that our references will speak well of us, some will be better than others. If these are people you know well and who you *believe* will speak well of you, why not confirm it now and leverage that goodwill throughout your job search?

At the very start of your job search, you should identify as many potential references as possible. The more options, the better the odds of coming up with excellent references. At the beginning of your job search, excellent references, though important, are simply an added bonus. Your real agenda is to use these contacts as another resource within your overall networking strategy.

How to Approach Potential References

The process is simplicity itself. Start with an introduction that covers these essential points and gets you both on the same page: "John, this is _____. We worked together at Citibank between 2002 and 2006. How's it going?" It is appropriate here to catch up on gossip and the like. Then broach the subject of your call.

"John, I wanted to ask your advice. [*Everyone loves to be asked for an expert opinion.*] We've had some cutbacks at Fly-By-Night Finance, as you probably heard," or "The last five years at Bank of Crooks and Criminals International have been great, and the _____ project we are just winding down has been a fascinating job. Nevertheless, I've decided this would be a perfect time for a strategic career move to capitalize on my experience."

Then, "John, I realize how important references can be, and I was wondering if I might use you as a reference when the time comes." The response will usually be positive, but if not, it's better to find out now, rather than down the line when it could blow a job offer. Given a positive response, you can continue with, "Thanks, John, I hoped you would say that. Let me update you about what I have been doing recently and tell you about the type of job I'm after." Give a capsule description of what you've done since you worked together and, in talking about your job search goals, focus on what you can do, not what you want to do: *Talking too much about what you want in a dream job only reduces your chances of a reference, or any other networking contact, giving you leads.*

As you begin to wrap up the conversation, you might also ask John if he would take a look at your resume for you. There are two reasons for this:

1. It gets your resume in his hands so he can pass it on to others.

2. It gives you a reason to follow up with John in two or three weeks, when you can ask for job leads again.

Notice the goal is *not* to get feedback on your resume, although you often will. Instead, it's to get your resume in the contact's hands so that he might pass it on and so that you can call for feedback and follow up with questions about job leads.

Always say thank you for the help you receive and show appreciation by following up your call with a thank-you e-mail (see *Knock 'em Dead Job Search Letter Templates* for examples).

With the scene set in this manner, you can network with each of these potential references every month or two, either for input on a particular opportunity or to ask for other intelligence relevant to your search. This might include leads or information about a specific company; for example, "Tina, do you know anyone who went to work at _____?"

References as Referrals

References can represent great networking resources; everyone you ask to be a reference for you will be flattered, and because they think well of you and know of your transition from early in your job search, they are prime candidates to offer referrals and introductions for jobs at their current company or elsewhere.

Professional associations, alumni networks, and potential references offer you superb networking resources that are often overlooked by job hunters, and they also serve to increase your skills, perceived value, and *professional brand*. In the next chapter, we'll look at how to effectively tap into your community networks as well.

CHAPTER 11

PERSONAL AND COMMUNITY
NETWORKS

If your friends and family are like most people, they would like to help you with your job search, but often they just don't know how. This challenge calls for a new way to think about and leverage the personal and community networks we all share. While networking should become an integral part of your life, it will always move into higher gear when strategic career moves are on your front burner.

There are a wide variety of personal and community-based networks available to you, depending on your interests and your willingness to become an active member of your local community:

- *Some are personal*: family, friends, and service industry acquaintances. These tend to be the people you see on a regular basis.

- *Others are more formal and socially oriented*: spiritual, community, local business, and volunteer groups. These tend to be professional in nature but not restricted to a specific profession (Kiwanis, etc.), community-based groups that focus on a common interest (Big Brother, Big Sister), or spiritual or faith based. Membership in community-based groups gives you a potential bond based on your common commitment to community and shared interests. You can find out about these groups in your local newspapers, at the library, through a local school or church, or by searching online.

Personal Networks

The good news is that the people who know you best, your family and friends, will really try to help you. The bad news is that since most of them may have known you since you were a snot-nosed brat, you have been categorized, stereotyped, and pigeonholed. They might not really know—or might incorrectly guess—the nature of your career. Odds are they don't know what you are capable of doing or what you want to do. Case in point: After sixteen books and millions of copies sold, two optical patents, and a couple of other reasonably significant achievements, my immediate family is still genuinely surprised that I know to come in from the rain. These people aren't stupid, but unlike the contacts you make in your professional networks, they probably don't have a full grasp of what you do for a living. On the other hand, they are highly motivated to help you. It is easy to squander this potentially valuable resource by tapping into it before you have thought through how best to help your extended family help you.

Many job hunters make the mistake of confusing the members of this network by giving them too much information. With the right guidance, however, your immediate circle will cast a wide net and come up with leads for you, even if they have nothing to do with your professional world.

Here are the steps to help your loved ones help you:

1. Think carefully about what you do for a living and put it in a one- or two-sentence description that even Aunt Aggie can grasp: *"I am a computer programmer; I write the instructions that help computers run."*

2. Think carefully about the job you want, the kind of company you will work for, and the kind of people you need to talk to. Condense it into a one- or two-sentence explanation: *"I'm looking for a job with another computer company. It would be great if you or your friends knew anyone I could talk to who works with computers."* Keep it really simple.

3. Give them the information you need to get in touch with these people: *"I'm looking for the names, e-mail addresses, and telephone numbers of anyone in these areas* [but maybe don't confuse aging Aunt Aggie with e-mail talk]. *I'm not looking for someone to hire me; I'm just looking for people in my field with whom I can network."*

This process of breaking your networking needs into *just three* simple statements gives your immediate circle something they can really work with.

Community Networks

It's good to be involved in your local community, both for your own emotional health and for the health of your community. Your involvement will provide you with a richer personal life, as well as a wide array of networking opportunities. You will find that effective networking with these groups is a little more time-consuming than with professional groups; after all, you have no prior professional relationships, and they don't have a familial obligation to help you out.

At the same time, you can't possibly join all the groups your community has to offer, so you will have to make some decisions about what is practical and which activities are going to be valuable to you in and of themselves; if the activity is personally fulfilling, you are more likely to stick with it over time and reap the personal fulfillment and networking rewards that come from your involvement. These might comprise:

- **Service industry acquaintances.** Electricians, plumbers, carpenters, accountants, lawyers, hairdressers—anyone whose services you retain is a potential networking resource.
- **Spiritual/community/volunteer groups.** These groups connect you with people who wish to make a difference by reaching out to others. Participation in spiritual and volunteer communities helps us achieve a sense of meaning and balance in our lives, and such groups are especially helpful in the emotionally troubled times of job and career change.
- **Hobby or special-interest groups.** This could be a book club, a women's/men's group, a dance class, or any of the vast number of community-based special-interest groups. It doesn't matter, so long as the activity is one that energizes the inner you by taking you away from the worries of your professional world. The people you meet will likely have professional careers, and you can build a bond based on your shared interests.
- **Business, professional, or civic groups.** All communities have networks of professionals joined together in formal groups: Rotarians, Chamber of Commerce, Kiwanis, and many more. These community-based associations, societies, and clubs are professionally oriented in membership, but they aren't focused on one profession. They straddle the line between your professional and community-based networking

activities. These groups were conceived as networking tools; they give you another angle of attack for your job search, and perhaps improve your social life.

In your local community networking, your need for job leads should take a back seat to being involved as a productive member. Soon enough, you'll learn what people do for a living, while they learn about you both as a professional and as a human being. As opportunities arise, you can talk about your job search needs.

Your involvement in these groups will not only pay dividends for your job search, it will help you overcome the self-imposed isolation that many of us tend toward in times of uncertainty, and that is reason enough in itself to join.

Your Job Search Network

During a job search you can sometimes feel that companies are looking for everyone but you. This can get depressing at times, so you need to be aware of the emotion and manage it. One way is to join or create a local support group and job search network with people in the same situation, whether these are online or local community-based networks.

A number of national organizations and many communities support job search networks through religious or other social organizations. Members meet, usually on a weekly basis, to exchange ideas and job leads and, just as important, to share and laugh with others in transition.

You can find groups in your area online at *www.careerjournal .com*, *www.jobbankinfo.org*, or *www.rileyguide.com*. Your local state employment office also maintains lists of job search support groups.

Gathering Leads from Local Contacts

You never know whom you're going to meet at the grocery store, coffee shop, hairdresser, or gym. To network effectively in these situations, you need a "networking mindset" that you can get into at a moment's notice. With a networking mindset, you will be surprised at the range of useful people you will meet. Even if they know nothing about your profession, they might know someone involved in the same field as you. Everyone you meet has the potential to know someone who can be useful to your job search.

You can network with people you meet at conventions, association meetings, class reunions, fundraisers, the gym, the coffee shop, continuing-education classes, or at community, social, spiritual, and sporting events. You can talk to them over the telephone, by letter, or via e-mail, online chat, or message posting. While the information-gathering aspects of these conversations will remain fairly constant regardless of the communication medium, there are one or two unique considerations about networking in person.

In-Person Networking

As you never know when you are going to make useful contacts, always maintain a well-put-together appearance in your local community. That doesn't mean that you always have to be dressed for a job interview, just that you should give consideration to your appearance.

You have to make the effort to reach out to others, and that means working out how you will introduce yourself; at the tennis class, for example: "Hello, I'd like to introduce myself. My name is Mark Germino. I just started playing tennis. How about you?" Always try to end with a question that encourages your contact to introduce and talk about herself. Once there has been a conversational exchange, you can begin to move forward with your networking agenda, perhaps by saying what you do. Say, "I'm in accounting, how about you?" rather than plunging into a detailed description of your situation.

Keep It Short

Even though gatherings of associations, clubs, and societies provide excellent networking opportunities, they are not scheduled specifically for that activity. Try to keep your initial in-person networking conversations to less than five minutes. You don't want to be known as an overly talkative bore. You can end a conversation gracefully with an offer of your business card, and you should recognize that a request for your card is a signal for you both to move on. If someone you meet isn't carrying a card, have her write her name and contact information on the back of one of yours, and always try to get a telephone number and an e-mail address.

Whenever you meet someone in person, send an e-mail to say thanks for any helpful information you may have gathered from the conversation. It also serves to keep you on that person's radar.

Now let's look in more detail at the substance of these networking conversations, so that you can learn to get maximum leverage out of them.

PART III

YOUR SOCIAL NETWORK–
INTEGRATED JOB SEARCH

CHAPTER 12

FIRST GET ORGANIZED

With a logical and organized plan of attack for integrating social networking into all your job-hunting activities, you are more likely to have a successful job search. Your plans should include developing not only the ability to gather and disseminate information, but also the ability to access the information you have gathered in the future; think of it as professional recycling.

This probably isn't your first job search and it almost certainly won't be your last. Since the statistics predict between twelve and fifteen job and career changes throughout your work life, carefully storing and organizing the professionally relevant intelligence you capture during this job search will supply your next transition with a starting point far superior to anything you have at your fingertips today.

Developing greater control of the tools of job search and career management makes it more likely that you will be able to make future strategic career transitions on *your* timetable, rather than being caught flat-footed and unemployed by an unexpected layoff.

With a database of all the potential employers in your area (you'll learn how to do this in Chapter 14) and a wide range of networking contacts in six or more professionally focused networks (LinkedIn, Google+, Facebook, Twitter, and your alumni and professional associations), you'll have a powerful career management database and be in a position to more effectively guide your professional destiny.

Creating a Career Management Database

You start by building a database of all the job postings you have collected: both those job postings for the target jobs of your current search and those that will be shared with others as part of your social networking outreach. There are a couple of reasons for saving rather than deleting this information:

- Openings that aren't right for you still identify companies in your target geographic market. They also represent openings that could be just what peers and professional colleagues on *approximately* your level are eager to find. These companies will likely still be hiring these job titles over the next few years.
- The job postings that represent too-senior positions today still identify companies that historically have openings for the person you will grow into, and maybe in your next search these will be your ideal target jobs. When you store this information, you will be able to start that next search with lots of relevant leads. In the meanwhile, it's an intelligent strategy to offer these leads to people who can assist the progression of your career.

These are just two of the ways in which what you do today can help you become more proactive in guiding the path of your career and more successful over the long haul.

If you aren't organized with clear goals every day, the Internet will bury you in an avalanche of information, and you'll spin in circles like a dog chasing his tail and achieving just about as much. The long-term success of your professional life demands an organized place for your job search, ongoing professional development, and career management activities.

What Goes Into a Career Management Database?

In an increasingly uncertain world, where job security is a thing of the past, job search and career management skills will become ever more important for your professional survival. Building a career management database on your desktop now, and nurturing it over the long haul, is a critical component of your long-term survival and financial security.

In addition to job postings, you should create folders for target companies that gather together all the insights you unearth about that company and your contacts within it when they are not already captured as networking contacts on your social media sites. You should capture the same information about recruitment firms and your contacts within them.

Additions to your professional knowledge base should be made at the time they accrue. For example, when you establish contact with recruiters who work in your industry, save all details about the person and the company in a document, and store the document within the appropriate folder at the end of your day when you implement your Plan, Do, Review Cycle (see the Multitasking section of Chapter 2). If you don't capture the information for retrieval as you gather it, you'll remember it for a couple of days, but you'll have long forgotten everything when next you need it a year or two down the road. Organize yourself to capture information today that you can use throughout your work life and you create an important foundation for your future security.

Telephone Smarts

With a daily job search goal of *getting into conversation with the people who can hire you*, your phone is important. If you have a landline, most telephone companies allow you two or three alternate numbers at no extra charge with your basic service, and usually these come with a distinctive ring tone. This means you can have a dedicated line with a distinctive ring for all your job search and career management activities.

If, like many people today, you just use a cell phone, you can get cell phones with two incoming lines, each with a different number, and also have a dedicated line with a distinctive ring for all your job search and career management activities. These phones have long been popular in Asia but are just appearing on the scene in America. You can also get apps that turn your cell into a two-line phone. For example, Totemic Inc. has an app in the Apple iTunes store that adds a second line to your iPhone and turns your iPad/iPad Mini or iPod Touch into a full-featured phone wherever you're connected to the Internet via WiFi or 3G/4G/LTE.

If you don't have a two-line cell phone—and not many people do as yet—you'll need to make a commitment that for the duration of your search, you will always answer in a professional manner and forgo answering with your personal variations of, "Yo, wassup?" and "Yeah?", neither of which contribute much to a desirable *professional persona* or to the *professional brand* you are working to create.

Maximizing Time Usage

You have five days a week to execute your job search and you need to make every hour and every day productive. Networking and the tactics that we discuss in the following three chapters—how to leverage job banks and resume banks, direct approach, headhunters, and job fairs—are the most commonly used job search tactics and have proved themselves the most effective job interview generators. They all generate job interviews and job offers, but none of them is guaranteed when used exclusively, and any of them could be the one to deliver your next career opportunity.

That adds up to six activities: working with job banks and resume banks, direct approach to hiring executives, networking, headhunters, and job fairs. Job fairs won't take much of your time and headhunters are overly useful for networking purposes, so essentially you have four activities to integrate into a five-day workweek. You can alternate them from day to day or do one the first half of the day and the other after lunch.

Your best odds for achieving results are with different job search activities each day, with social networking tactics integrated into each (as we'll discuss throughout the remainder of the book). This will give you an approach that supercharges your job interview results.

Moving Forward

We have been talking throughout the book about the many exciting innovations that technology and social networking offer you. Now while you will benefit from applying these tactics to your job search, you can't afford to ignore the existence of other Internet-based tools for job search. Throughout the next four chapters, I'll share tactics to help you integrate these other effective job search approaches into an overall networked job search strategy. The results will empower you to double, triple, and quadruple the number of job interviews you generate. (To turn the job interviews you generate into job offers, you might want to check out *Knock 'em Dead Job Interview*.) To begin, we'll look at how best to leverage job sites and resume banks.

CHAPTER 13

JOB SITES AND RESUME BANKS

A man who goes fishing and puts one hook in the water has only one chance of catching any of the millions of fish in the sea, and one fish is the best he can ever do. A man with two hooks in the water has double the chances of landing a fish, and has also earned himself the opportunity to outperform the first guy by landing twice as many. The more hooks you have in the water, the better your chances of landing job interviews and job offers.

Employers prefer candidates who come to them directly or as a result of referrals, which makes networking a powerful and favored approach of job hunters everywhere. This means that your most effective approach to conducting a successful job search is to find ways to weave social networking tactics into every aspect of your search.

The Dangers of Job Site Noodling

With tens of thousands of job sites and resume banks, you could spend an eternity noodling around without getting anything done. The danger is that this aimless noodling can be highly addictive because it *feels* like you are searching for job opportunities, plus it involves zero rejection. Unfortunately, the long-term results of this unfocused noodling are decreasing self-confidence and increasing depression due to lack of results. The Internet increases your ability to gather and disseminate information, but your responsibility is to understand and control this tendency, and not allow yourself to be mesmerized by a world of endless clicking. Every day of your job search, your primary goal should be to *get into conversation with the people with the authority to hire you*, or the people who can introduce you to them, for the high-value job titles we have discussed throughout the book.

How to Identify Worthwhile Job Sites

There are so many thousands of job sites that you could never hope to visit them all, and so you start by identifying sites that are relevant to your search.

Does the site have job postings that are suitable for you? If it doesn't, you can move on to the next site; if it does, you will want to register with the site and receive job alerts in your e-mail when new jobs matching your requested criteria get posted to the site. This way you will be notified of suitable jobs rather than wasting time searching the site for them on a regular basis.

Job Site Priorities: The Paying Customers

Most job sites, except for some executive sites, are free: It's the employers who are paying to post their job openings and to search the resume database. Consequently, job sites work with employers to develop ever-more-efficient screening tools. It's important that you be aware of this when setting up your account and filling out a profile: the part of registration that makes you discoverable to corporate recruiters and headhunters.

Job Site Registration and Profile Creation

Most job sites break up the registration/profile-building/resume-uploading process into a number of steps. These steps typically include providing information on topics like Target Job, Profile Summary, Skills, Work Experience, Relocation, Salary, Ideal Job, Education, etc. Not too difficult, as these are pretty much the topics you have already addressed in creating both your social media profiles and your resume.

Target Job Title
Use the target job title you determined with your TJD (Target Job Deconstruction) exercise. If you found a number of common variations of your job title, it can help increase your discoverability to include those variations.

Job Objective/Career Summary
If a job site uses Job Objective as a category be very careful what you write, because no one is interested in what you want at this stage of the recruitment cycle, so writing about your wishes at this point only wastes space. Additionally, what you want is unlikely to be in a recruiter's database search terms, so this won't help your discoverability either.

Whether this section of the registration is labeled Career Summary or Job Objective, this is the place to capture your ability to deliver on the requirements of your target job. In the *Knock 'em Dead* approach to resume creation (*Knock 'em Dead Resume Templates*) and acing job interviews (*Knock 'em Dead Job Interview* and

Knock 'em Dead: The Ultimate Job Search Guide) we talk about creating something we call a Performance Profile: three to six short sentences that reflect employer priorities for this job (as determined by the TJD process) and capture your professional capabilities in executing these priorities. This is the perfect information to increase your discoverability, because it reflects your credentials as they match employers' skill and experience priorities for this job, plus the terms they use to describe the job.

The dialogue box for this section often has lots of space, so you can end it by inserting a header that says, "The opportunity to use these skills." Then paste in the entire collection of professional skills that you discovered in the TJD exercise and listed on your resume and social media profiles as Professional Skills. While there is a section later in the registration for exactly this topic, putting in a full list of your professional skills here is both relevant to potential readers and doubles the amount of keywords in your profile that recruiters are likely to search for, thereby increasing your discoverability.

Salary Requirements

It is always better to give a range rather than a single figure and always easier to negotiate down rather than up. You can learn more about how to determine a realistic salary range and how to negotiate an offer in *Knock 'em Dead Job Interview.*

Ideal Job

If a category of Ideal Job is available, understand that no recruiter is remotely interested in your ideal job, and all you will achieve by discussing it here is a reduction of your discoverability.

In reality, your ideal job, and the one you are most likely to land and subsequently be successful in, is the job you are doing now. As such, you write, "The opportunity to . . ." and then follow with the same information that you used in the Career

Summary/Job Objective section (though worded slightly differently for readability). End with, " . . . and the opportunity to use these skills . . ." You then finish off by listing your professional skills once again.

This will support your discoverability by matching your skills and desires with employer priorities for this job, and by repeating for the second or third time the keywords that a recruiter is likely to use, you further increase your discoverability. Test to see if there is more space by pasting in your professional skills yet again. No one will actually read the repetition (and if they did, they would regard it as a glitch), but the software will catch and reward you for it by increasing your ranking in the search results.

Professional Experience

You can cut the information developed for your social media profiles or resume and paste it here, repeating your professional skills in the context of the jobs in which they were used.

Education

Education is the area most prone to exaggeration and outright lies, but for that very reason educational claims *can and do get checked*. Untruths can cause offers to be withdrawn and jobs to be terminated. Don't fake it.

Lack of a degree—and there are lots of valid reasons why you might not have one—bars you from contention for an increasing number of professional opportunities, but don't throw up your hands in despair. If you are involved in the pursuit of any post-secondary degree but haven't yet achieved it, you can still use it. Just state the school and the degree, adding a projected graduation date. This can often help you over the "lacks a degree" hurdle.

Note that you can do this as long as you are enrolled in at least one course toward that degree. Your pursuit of an education while you work is a plus in employers' eyes, and you have a right to show it to them and to show yourself in the best light.

Relocation

When completing questions about relocation, your answer is basically: "Open for the right opportunity." This is because:

1. It increases opportunity.
2. You can always say "no," but you can't say "yes" unless you've been asked.
3. For the right job, opportunity, and money, we would all move to Possum Trot, Kentucky (yes, there is such a place, and very beautiful it is too).
4. Any job you interview for but reject will only improve your interviewing chops, which is both your most important and probably your very weakest professional skill, because of your lack of experience in turning job interviews into job offers.
5. It gives you leads to share in your networking initiatives.

Name Dropping

Recruiters often look for candidates who either are working for or have worked for certain companies or on certain accounts/brands. If you have worked for "name" companies and products, drop those names—in this profile, and in all your social media profiles and your resume. You can also drop corporate names and brand names if you have been a vendor, contractor, or client.

Define Your Job Search Needs

When you are asked to define the jobs that interest you, set your sights wide. You may get too many responses initially, but you can gradually narrow the parameters. It's better to plow through a little junk than miss a great opportunity. Alternatively, you might not be getting enough responses from a particular site and may want to recast your needs in broader terms.

Responding to Job Postings

Whenever you respond to a job posting, do exactly as requested, but also copy the job posting and all contact information for that company to a folder on your desktop. You will need this if an interview occurs. In addition, you can cross-reference the job posting with people in your various networks and perhaps come up with a name and a high-value job title to which you can send the resume directly, or someone who might give you an introduction. Approaching the company in two different ways—and leveraging your social networking contacts in the process—doubles your chances of getting an interview.

If you choose your job sites well, you'll collect two types of job postings: opportunities that are good for you, and opportunities that might be perfect for the high-value job titles that you target as members of your professional networks: those people one to three levels above you, holding the same title, one level below you, or who interact with your title on a regular basis.

Before you file any job postings that are suitable for you, go through them carefully, looking for keywords that describe skill sets you have that are not captured in your existing resume and social media profiles. List these new terms for skill sets you possess in a Word document; you'll use this document to refresh your social media profiles (and your resume as it is posted in the resume banks), and in the process you will enhance your discoverability (more on this shortly).

Make a folder for each relevant site you visit, and store postings in one of the two folders—either for you or for sharing with network contacts. You'll quickly see which sites are most productive for you.

Finding More Hidden Jobs

You can leverage job sites in other ways too. Go to any job site and search its posted openings by putting in minimal keywords and restrictions. For example, if you were an insurance sales manager, you might try a simple keyword search for "insurance"; there may be hundreds of results, but the vast majority will be for insurance jobs other than the one you want. However, those results will reveal relevant recruiters and companies in your profession and target location—plus these opportunities will be perfect for your high-value networking contacts. These leads will become even more useful as we begin to leverage them using other little-known job search tactics and integrate them with social networking.

Companies all use their own websites as recruitment vehicles, and invariably have all open jobs posted there. So whenever you identify fresh companies in your target location, you should always visit their websites to see if there are suitable job openings posted there. Even if they do not have jobs for someone like you posted, you should still upload your resume. You don't really know what is going on at that company, and at the very least you will be in their database and become more readily discoverable when a need does arise.

If a company is looking for anyone even remotely connected with your area of professional expertise, they could also be looking for someone like you. This means you should then upload your resume and capture any contact information you can find to help research the company and perhaps approach the appropriate hiring managers directly or through networked referrals.

Resume Databases

When a job site has postings suitable for you, it means that recruiters will also be cruising that site's resume bank for candidates. This means that you will want to upload your resume. Some considerations to bear in mind:

1. Resume banks have purge dates, mostly so the recruiters who pay for access can be assured that they are not looking at stale resumes. The purge usually happens every ninety days; you will want to bear the dates in mind so that you can refresh your resume before then.

2. Recruiters also have the ability to restrict their searches by the date a resume was loaded; for example, they might want to restrict a search to resumes uploaded since their last visit—say, ten days ago.

3. With resume banks where you want to maintain the highest visibility, go in once a week and update your resume with new keywords you have identified in other job postings (the ones you noted in the Word document discussed a few paragraphs back). Make any change to your resume and the database search engine will recognize it as a brand new document.

4. When there are no new words with which to refresh your resume, you can achieve the same effect quite simply: Log in to your account, open your resume, replace a couple of words with a string of x's, and log out. Take a couple of deep breaths, log in again, replace the x's with the original words, and log out again. As far as the database search engine is concerned, you now have a brand new document.

Reading the latest edition of *Knock 'em Dead: The Ultimate Job Search Guide* will give you additional and more detailed tactics for getting the most mileage out of your chosen job sites and resume banks. We don't have the space in this book, and need to stay focused on leveraging your social networks. This we will continue to do in the next chapter, as we begin to look at direct research.

CHAPTER 14

DIRECT APPROACH TO
TARGET COMPANIES

Everything in a successful job search is geared toward *getting into conversations with the high-value job titles who have the authority to hire you*, and failing that, the people who know and work with them. As we have noted, these titles are typically people one to three title levels above your own, or people who are otherwise closely involved in the selection cycle.

There will be times when you can't find the right names and titles through your social networks—especially when you first start getting serious about building social networks and they aren't extensive enough. Additionally, the higher up the corporate ladder of success your high-value job titles are placed, the less likely it is that these executives are visible or readily accessible through social networking. As a consequence, in this chapter we'll look at alternative ways to connect with potential employers in your target geographic market, and the right names and titles to target within those companies. You can then work back through each of your networks for someone who can give you a referral or an introduction to otherwise inaccessible executives.

We'll begin by discussing tactics to ensure that you know of all the potential employers within commuting distance, and then move on to a number of different ways to identify high-value job titles.

How to Identify Potential Employers

You will never identify all the employers and all the jobs that are suitable for you and located within commuting distance by visiting job sites and networking. Sometimes you have to reverse engineer your job search strategy with these steps:

- Identify all the employers within your commuting range
- Visit their websites and check for jobs and high-value titles
- Upload your resume, whether or not there are suitable jobs posted
- Cross-reference each of those companies with networking contacts in each of the six major social networks, looking for contacts who work or have worked there

How to Identify Employers Within Commuting Distance
There are a number of ways to identify all the potential employers in your area:

- Search job sites with a variety of job titles common to your area of professional expertise. As you identify employers, visit each of their websites to look for jobs and to upload your resume. Don't forget to add them to a potential employers folder in your career management database; this procedure of capturing the information for future retrieval applies to most of the following points.

- Search job sites for jobs using just your target job title, then your professional or industry sector, your city, county, state, and the variety of zip codes that cover your target market. This will give you a longer list of employers. You'll visit each of their websites to look for jobs and, as appropriate, upload your resume.

- Use the job aggregator sites like Indeed.com and SimplyHired .com whose search engines scan thousands of sites looking for your search terms. Again, you can search by your target job title, then your professional or industry sector, your city, county, state, the variety of zip codes that cover your target market, and other database search term variations as we have discussed throughout the book.

- Search LinkedIn, Google+, Facebook, Twitter, and your professional and alumni networks using the same variety of search terms.

- You can use the apps and dashboard tools available on all your social media sites to search for job postings, and where applicable, employer pages by name, city, county, state, and zip codes.

- You can find lists of employers on your local Chamber of Commerce website.

- You can identify every publicly traded company in the world through the Standard & Poor's (S&P) website (a fee service) or through the S&P reference books at your local library (free). These include the names and titles of VPs and C-level management.

- Zapdata, owned by Dun & Bradstreet (D&B) is the online version of the D&B Million Dollar Directory (fee based), which you can also find for free in the public library. It contains data on over 15 million U.S. private and publicly held corporations. Includes names and titles of key executives.

Note: Your alumni and college career services, and some libraries, may be able to give you free online access to the S&P and Zapdata databases, and possibly useful research databases.

- You can find an extensive list of companies by industry on LinkedIn at *www.LinkedIn.com/companyDir?industries=*. When you find a relevant employer in your target location, link directly to that company's LinkedIn page.

Note: Not only is this an important step toward a direct approach, you can also look at who is following the company and commenting on their posts. This is useful for expanding your network with other committed professionals in the same field. You should then "like" their comments and link to them. This works on LinkedIn and on your other social media platforms.

- You can also use Google.com, Bing.com, and other search engines to look for job titles in your target market, or just potential employers. For instance, if you were looking for a job in the vicinity of Raleigh, NC, you could use phrases like, "Inc., Raleigh, N.C.," "Company, Raleigh, N.C.," "LLC, Raleigh, N.C.," and "Partners, Raleigh, N.C." You could also try variations of the above with a zip code, like "LLC 31405," or use zip codes relevant to your search parameters, like "Employers in 31405." All these variations will generate more lists of employers within your commuting parameters.

- You can also use all these search terms on each of your social networking platforms and the job sites you visit.

Google/Bing Alerts

With "Alerts" from any search engine, you can keep track of news on any topic that interests you, and in the process identify employers and often inside information about those employers, giving you ammunition for a well-considered approach. You can set up alerts for any topic using *www.google.com/alerts* or any other search engine. In a job search this could mean:

- Jobs with specific titles or the names of cities, counties, states, zip codes, or any of the other suggested tactics
- News about your profession or job title
- News about specific companies or people
- News about high-value titles at specific companies or in specific locations
- News about "stock splits"—this often indicates company growth
- News about "companies," "growing," "hiring"
- News about "contracts landed"—adding in the other search terms, "Contracts landed Atlanta," or "Contracts landed 45672," etc.

Use some of the great job search apps mentioned in the last few chapters using these same techniques.

After you decide on an Alert topic, you should then think about the channels where you want Google to search for this information: Everything, News, Books, Blogs, Video, Discussions, Applications, and more.

Bing and all the other search engines have similar tools that work in pretty much the same way, but because each search engine is built differently, they will all generate somewhat different results.

New Ways to Identify High-Value Job Titles

Once you have a comprehensive list of employers within commuting distance, you can start identifying high-value job titles. For the moment we'll leave networking contacts as a resource to fall back on while we develop some new approaches to identifying high-value names and titles that we may subsequently be able to approach directly and turn into networking contacts for the future. Alternatively, we can cross-reference such names, titles, and employers with our contacts in our six major social networks for introductions.

Who to Target in Your Job Search

We have already said that the hiring titles to target during your social networking and job search activities are usually people one to three titles above your target job, because these are the people most likely to be in a position to hire you. We also know that other titles likely to be involved in the selection process include management titles (again, one to three levels above you) in departments that have ongoing interaction with your department, peers holding similar titles to that for which you're applying, colleagues in departments that regularly interact with your department, and internal recruiters and HR professionals.

In fact, any name at one of the employers within your commuting radius is better than no name, and with the Internet at your fingertips there is endless opportunity to identify the names of people who carry either the job titles that would give them the authority to hire you, or titles that can tell you whom to talk to, or at least get you one step closer.

Sometimes those job titles one to three levels above yours aren't enough. Sometimes, your job and the corporate structure that towers over it can make for upward of half a dozen pitches to a target company, just to ensure that all the right people know you are available.

For example, let's say you are a young engineer crazy for a job with Last Chance Electronics. It is well within the bounds of reason that any or all of the following job titles could hold responsibility for, or be involved with the selection of, your job title, or at the very least could be knowledgeable about what is going on with recruitment in your area of professional expertise:

- Vice President of Engineering
- Chief Engineer
- Engineering Design Manager
- Vice President of Human Resources
- Technical Engineering Recruitment Manager
- Technical Recruiter
- Company President

Apply this thinking to your title and situation, thinking through all the titles that could be suitable for approach in a larger company, then use your networks and the other tactics we've discussed to identify the names that go with each of these titles at a targeted company. The more options you have, the more approaches you can make and the more results you will get, especially when you approach each potential hiring authority in a sequence of different ways, as we'll discuss over the coming pages.

Always strive to identify and get into a conversation with anyone who holds any of these types of high-value hiring titles at any and every company in your area, because getting into these conversations is the shortest path to job interviews, job offers, and getting the hell past the misery of this job search. This "direct approach" tactic is an essential element of your job search strategy.

How to Find High-Value Job Titles

There are a number of different tactics you can use to locate high-value titles relevant to your job search goals:

- Use different versions and combinations of your high-value job titles as search terms with Google and other search engines, such as the acronym, the full phrase, and variations for each of your high-value titles. For example: Chief Marketing Officer, CMO, and C.M.O. You might also try misspellings of these target titles; for instance, "M" is next to "N" on the keyboard and a common typo.

- Use quotation marks around words and phrases to help weed out irrelevant information. For example, if you had an alert for Accounting Manager, you would get alerts for that phrase and also alerts any time the word *Accounting* or the word *Manager* appeared on the Internet. You can work around this problem by putting quotation marks around the important phrase—"Accounting Manager."

- If there are variations on the job title—Accounting Manager, Manager of Accounting, Manager Accounts, Director Accounting, etc.—you should use "OR" in capital letters: "Accounting Manager OR Manager of Accounting OR Manager Accounts OR Director Accounting." Alternatively, you could do different searches for each.

- If you want to add geographic restrictions—say you only want to hear about jobs in Carle Place or Huntington, NY—put this second choice in parentheses: "Carle Place (OR Huntington, NY)."

- You can search for similar words and phrases by adding the tilde sign: ~. This functions as a symbol for "similar to," so with a phrase like "~accounting jobs," you might get finance jobs in your results. Be sure not to leave a space between the tilde (the squiggly thingy) and the word in question, or the search won't work.

  For example: A professional in pharmaceutical sales looking to make direct contact with hiring authorities for a job at a specific company in the Pittsburgh area could try all the following keyword searches and gather new usable information on each search. Try it yourself, first as a Google Search, then as a Google News search:

- "Pharmaceutical sales"
- "Sales (OR Account Manager) (OR District Manager)" Pennsylvania (OR Pittsburgh)
- "Sales Manager" _____ [*company name*] Pennsylvania (OR Pittsburgh)
- "Director Sales" _____ [*company name*] Pennsylvania (OR Pittsburgh)
- "Vice President (OR VP OR V.P.) Sales" _____ [*company name*] Pennsylvania (OR Pittsburgh)
- "~Sales Manager" Pharmaceutical (OR Pharma) Pennsylvania (OR Pittsburgh)

You could also:

- Repeat all without "pharmaceutical"
- Repeat all without company name
- Repeat all with just variations on the job title
- Repeat all with separate searches for target title plus: hired, resigned, and deceased

Try these and other keyword phrases suitable to your needs and you will come up with a wide range of job openings, companies, job sites, and recruiters. Just remember that the results on the first pages of a Google search are only those of companies that have spent time and money to ensure high search engine rankings. Continue to dig down in your search results and you'll begin to stumble across people who hold these and similar job titles, usually linked to one of their social media profiles.

- Check out the company website. On the "about us" pages, you can sometimes find names and titles of management.
- Call the company and ask for the name of the titleholder. This may sound old-fashioned, but it works.

Other Online Resources

There are other online resources that can be valuable supplements to the information you get from your personal and professional networks. Sites such as *www.vault.com* will tell you what past and current employees think about their employer. Other online resources such as *www.wetfeet.com* will give you great info about your target companies, as will the contacts in your networks.

These searches will provide useful background information for pitching, and during interviews your homework will be evident. This is always flattering to the interviewer, who sees you've paid attention to detail and shown effort and enthusiasm, each of which can end up being deciding factors in a tight job race. As you develop folders of information on potential employers, be sure to capture the details so that you have retrievable insights for this job search and for future strategic career moves.

Here are some other online resources for researching companies and identifying management titleholders:

*www.virtualpet.com/industry
/howto/search.htm*
www.standardandpoors.com
www.idexec.com
www.zapdata.com
www.hoovers.com
www.quintcareers.com
www.vault.com
www.infousa.com
www.thomasnet.com

www.superpages.com
www.jigsaw.com
www.zoominfo.com
*www.corporateinformation
.com*
www.ceoexpress.com
www.infospace.com
www.search-it-all.com
www.searchbug.com

More Resources for Finding the Names of Hiring Authorities

The resources available reach to the horizon. Standard & Poor's also has a far less well-known database of executives by name and title: a Biographical Directory/Database that delivers some amazingly detailed personal information. These higher-level titles will be identifiable through one of the above resources or through one of the following options:

www.onesource.com
www.knowx.com
www.jigsaw.com
www.lead411.com/about.html
www.business.com/directory/advertising_and_marketing/sales/selling_techniques/lead_generation/

Employee Referral Programs

An increasingly popular recruitment tool is the incentivizing of referrals from employees with corporate Employee Referral Programs, which typically offer a monetary reward for successfully referring employees to the company.

When you have a list of particularly desirable employers, it might be worth doing a few database searches for phrases like "[company name] referral program." If a company has an employee referral program, it can encourage a networking contact to act as a referral for you. This won't work all the time, but when your target is a highly desirable employer, it might be worth the effort.

Don't Approach Dream Employers Too Soon

As you engage in this potential employer research, your database of potential employers within your commuting distance will grow exponentially, and you may also want to create a folder of dream employers in your career management database.

If you are just starting a job search, build the information in these folders and beware of applying for jobs with these "superdesirable" employers right away, even when you have networking contacts who can open doors for you.

I'm sure you sometimes hear about the hit shows on Broadway, but what you may not know is that these shows don't actually start on Broadway: They go through months of rehearsals, previews with selected audiences, and then road trips to cities around the country to iron out the wrinkles. They do this because they don't want to screw up when they open on "the Great White Way"—the most important stage in the world. These experts in seamless performance understand that it doesn't just happen, that we make mistakes and have to iron them out, and that this takes a little time and effort.

This analogy has implications for your job search. Of all the professional skills that are important to landing your next step, your ability to turn job interviews into job offers is both the most important and, at the same time, almost certainly your weakest skill, because you have very little experience and skill in this area. In the early days of a job search, your social media platform, resume, and interviewing skills are probably still in the development and retooling phases, and almost certainly not up to speed. The last thing you need to do is land an interview at the company of your dreams and then screw it up because interview nerves make you trip over your tongue.

It is better to hold off on applying to your dream companies for a few weeks, until you know that your social media profiles and your resume focus on the same target job and reflect complementary messaging. Meanwhile, you can land a couple of interviews and learn not to swallow your tongue in the first few minutes, better preparing you to meet with the people at a dream employer.

All this research has obvious immediate value, but it has significant long-term value as well, because you are building a personalized reference work on your industry/specialty/profession that will help you throughout the twists and turns of a long career.

We'll now turn to developing the best ways to leverage visits to local and virtual job fairs, and integrate the experiences with your overall social networking strategy.

CHAPTER 15

JOB FAIRS

Job fairs (also called "career fairs" or "career days") are occasions on which actively hiring companies get together, usually under the auspices of a job fair promoter, to attract large numbers of potential employees. On a college campus the promoter is invariably Career Services. Job fairs can take place both locally and online as virtual job fairs. Live job fairs are usually one-day-only events, while virtual job fairs have greater flexibility.

Though they're often regarded as events only relevant to entry- and lower-level workers, you'll see by the end of this chapter that job fairs can be useful to professionals at most levels of experience.

Live Job Fairs

Except in times of high employment, live local job fairs aren't regular events, so they won't take up much of your time; still, you should become an active participant when they do occur.

Live fairs often charge a small entrance fee, but in return you get direct access to all the employers, plus formal presentations by company representatives and local employment experts. When you organize yourself properly, take the right attitude, and work all the opportunities, job fairs can generate plenty of valuable job leads and contacts for your social networks.

Very few people actually get hired at job fairs; for most companies, job fairs are attractive when they are in an expansion mode and have multiple job openings now or in the immediate future. For employers, the exercise is one of collecting resumes so that screening and meaningful meetings can take place in the ensuing days and weeks. Nevertheless, you should be "on" at all times, because serious interviews do occur on the spot.

What to Bring

When you attend job fairs, go prepared with:

PROPER BUSINESS ATTIRE

You may be meeting your new boss, and you don't want the first impression to be less than professional.

BUSINESS CARDS

If you are currently employed, remember to request discretion and confidentiality. If you are in transition you might also consider having some business cards made; you can get 250 for as little as $10 at *www.VistaPrint.com*. Don't make the card fussy by choice of paper stock, gloss, or graphics: Simple and understated makes the strongest professional impression.

Business cards are an accepted sales tool the world over, and while a job hunter will obviously take resumes to a job fair, a business card is an additional marketing tool for such an event. When you are not attending a job fair, they're also much less intrusive than carrying around a wad of resumes under your arm.

If you are unemployed, you can quite easily turn a business card into a miniaturized resume. If you want to try a business card resume, consider the severely limited space available to you and use that space wisely. You need to:

1. Communicate critical information: your name, your target job title, your job's number one deliverable, and contact information.
2. Use legible, businesslike fonts, such as Times Roman and Arial.
3. Make it readable. Limit the word count so that you can maximize font size to increase readability. No one in a position to hire you can read an 8-point font . . . and reminding someone that they are aging and have failing eyesight—not such smart positioning for your sales pitch.
4. Make a strong performance statement. As we decided earlier, the number one deliverable in your job (and all jobs) is the *identification, prevention, and solution of problems* within your area of professional expertise; this is ultimately what we all get hired to do. Notice in the following example that by starting the performance statement with a verb, you not only demonstrate an understanding of what is at the heart of your job, you also deliver a powerful personal brand statement by telling the reader what you deliver.

For instance, an accounting professional who works in Accounts Receivable might have a transitional business card resume that looks something like this:

Martin Yate   516.555.3728
Accounts Receivable Accountant
Focused on the prevention and solution of recurrent A/R problems
Top.Accountant11579@gmail.com
http://www.LinkedIn.com/topaccountant

Notice how many of the tactics we have discussed throughout the book come together in the limited space available with a business card to tell a convincing story in very few words.

RESUMES

You should take as many copies of your resume as there are exhibitors, times two. You'll need one to leave at the exhibit booth, and an additional copy for anyone you have a meaningful networking conversation with. If you have resumes targeted to different jobs, take copies of all of them.

LAPTOP, TABLET, OR SMARTPHONE

You need a means of capturing useful job search intelligence. If you take your laptop, tablet, or smartphone, you'll also have the ability to do emergency research as circumstances demand.

Social Networking

Job fairs offer a great opportunity for social networking with other professionals as well. Almost anyone you meet at a local job fair is a professional who lives in the area too, so you should make the effort to speak to other attendees as you walk around. Introduce yourself, smile, share what you do and ask your contact for similar information, exchange contact information, and make a commitment to share leads and connect through your social networks.

If you know other people going to a job fair in advance (perhaps you are a member of a job search support group), you should go with a collaborative effort in mind. Put the word out about the job fair and your attendance through all your social networking groups, and if you are on Twitter you might also try spreading the word with #jobfair and #careerfair. Your goal with a job fair, apart from the obvious, is to connect with other local professionals and build your networks. These people may be in different professions, but if, as a group, you establish what you are each looking for and you all make the effort to speak to and collect business cards from corporate recruiters and other attendees regardless of their profession, you can help one another find more leads.

Arrange to meet at the end of the day to exchange leads. I have witnessed this in action: I've seen a group of twenty who were total strangers in the morning happily exchanging handfuls of leads and business cards at the end of the day. Think of it as live crowdsourcing.

Visit Every Booth

It's easy to walk into a job fair and be drawn like a moth to the biggest and most attractive booths, sponsored by the largest and most established companies, and ignore the lesser ones. Remember that *small companies, with less than 500 employees, generate the majority of jobs in America*, and many of these jobs are generated by companies in their first ten years of existence. Because of this, you should work your way through the job fair methodically, visiting every booth, not just the ones with the flashing lights and all the moths fluttering around.

Have an Agenda

Attend with specific objectives in mind:

- **Talk to someone at every booth.** You can walk up and ask questions about company activities, and whom they are looking for, before you talk about yourself. This allows you to present yourself in the most relevant light.
- **Collect business cards** from every company representative you speak to so you can follow up with an e-mail and a call when they are not so harried. As company staff will be involved in recruitment, you should also reach out to them for connections on each of your social networking platforms.

- **Pitch or don't pitch.** If you have a background and resume that make you a match for a specific opportunity, make your pitch. If, on the other hand, there's a job you can do but your resume needs some adaptation to better position your candidacy, take a different approach. By all means pitch the company representative, but don't hand over a resume that will detract from your candidacy. You might suggest that you have run out and will send one. Then get the contact's business card and e-mail address in order to follow up with a resume customized to the opportunity.

- **Collect company brochures and collateral materials.**

- **Arrange times and dates to follow up** with as many employers as possible: "Ms. Jones, I realize you are very busy today, and I would like to speak to you further. Your opportunities at _____ sound exactly suited to my skills and interests. I would like to set up a time when we could talk about _____ (job title)."

In addition to the exhibit hall, there will be group presentations by employers. As all speakers love feedback, move in when the crush of presenter groupies has died down. You will have more knowledge of the company and the time to customize your pitch to the needs and interests of the employer, plus you'll get more time and closer attention.

On leaving each booth, and at the end of the day, go through your notes while everything is still fresh in your mind. Review each company and what possibilities it may hold for you. Also review what you have learned about industry trends, new skill requirements, marketplace shifts, and long-term staffing needs. Plan to send e-mails and make follow-up calls within the week to everyone with whom you spoke.

Job fairs provide the best opportunities for administrative, professional, and technical people. However, this doesn't mean middle management and executive staff can't gather information, collect cards, and generate leads (more on this shortly).

Virtual Career Fairs

Virtual job fairs are on the rise because they are cheaper and reach wider audiences. Google "job fair" and "career fair" and, as these can be metropolitan, regional, or national in nature, do additional searches adding your city, state, and region.

With a virtual job fair, you will need to fill out your profile and upload your resume, just as you do with social networking sites. You do this so that job fair clients can subsequently search the database of attendees for potential employees. You'll need a headshot for your profile, and it's a great timesaver to keep a copy of your profile in a Microsoft Word document within your career management folder, so that it is ready to cut and paste in situations like this. Your approach to a virtual job fair is very similar to the way you would approach a live one: You will want to speak to someone at every company that is part of the fair—at least to the extent that you can post a question and get a recruiter's response. Virtual fairs can take place on a specific day, but often they are open and staffed for up to a week and sometimes a month afterward, with recruiters accessing the database for longer still.

Reaching Out to Company Representatives

A big plus is that company contact names are either posted or readily available, so while you may not get into e-mail, chat, telephone, or Skype conversations with the titles who have the authority to hire you, you will be able to get into conversations with people who are involved in the recruitment and selection cycle, and who know and can introduce you to the high-value names and titles likely to hire someone like you.

Chat Rooms

At virtual job fairs, both recruiters and hiring managers are often available in the chat rooms, so you will want to visit each company's "booth" *and* their chat room. While you may get into an e-mail exchange subsequent to your visit, you can usually get into a live chat immediately, and this is very close to holding those desirable live conversations. I have heard of recruiters asking on the spot for a Skype number to initiate an immediate face-to-face meeting. This means that you need to understand how Skype interviews work.

Skype Interviews

Skype is the fastest, cheapest telecommunications service available, and it has the best voice quality. If you don't have a Skype account, set one up now (free to set up and as little as $2.99 a month to maintain), because the odds of someone wanting to interview over Skype increases daily.

The call can be a simple telephone call or it can be a video call. Recruiters usually want to do video, and this affects how you should dress when attending virtual job fairs.

As I write this, I've just returned from my morning bike ride. I wanted to get the words flowing immediately, so I haven't shaved yet and I'm wearing shorts and a T-shirt and generally look like I've been dragged through a hedge backward. This doesn't affect my subject-matter expertise, but I sure don't look like a career expert. It is fine for me to dress like a bum when I'm sitting alone typing on my Mac, but if I thought there was a possibility of a Skype interview in my day, I would dress and prepare my environment for it.

Skype Video Meetings

With a Skype video meeting, you simply download the program, open the icon on your desktop, and call a number. You can also enable the video option as needed. If video is at all likely, you need to dress at least semi-professionally. When I have Skype meetings and am not dressed appropriately for the occasion, I simply stick something over my laptop's built-in camera. You could do the same, and if questioned on this, you have my permission to tell a white lie: "I must have some kind of bug because I just can't get the video function to work today. Would you like to reschedule for when I have the issue fixed?" Most of the time the recruiter will want to proceed with the meeting, and if not, you will have avoided making a bad first impression.

I've done a lot of TV over the years, and will never get over my shock and amusement at those oh-so-immaculately-dressed anchors sitting behind their desks. I'd go on set and be introduced to a show's host, who'd be wearing a thousand-dollar suit jacket, shirt, and tie, but I can't tell you how many times he would be wearing shorts or jeans. The moral of the story is that all you need do for Skype interviews is dress for "above the desk."

Your Skype Set

If you are on video, it will be a head-and-shoulders close-up with the area behind you framing the shot. Think about where you will be doing the interview and what will be behind you: a plain blank wall is usually the best option.

Your Skype Performance

I do media all the time, and even with all my on-camera experience, what I am going to tell you still took me a while to figure out.

When you talk to someone on Skype, you tend to look at the person onscreen and not the camera lens on top of your laptop or tablet. This is a mistake. From the other end of the line you are seen to be looking down and can appear to be avoiding eye contact—not the impression you want to create.

The camera lens is usually in the top center of your laptop/tablet; if not, you will need to clip a separate lens to the top of your device. This means the simple solution is to put your laptop on a pile of books so that the lens on your device is at about eye level and looking straight at your face.

Train yourself to look into the lens, not at the interviewer's onscreen image. Imagine that the lens represents the interviewer's eyes; look straight into it and smile as you talk, just as you would in normal conversation. What the interviewer will experience is a warm and confident candidate who isn't afraid to make eye contact. This may take some practice, but job searches are going to increasingly use Skype for screening interviews, so it's worth taking the time to get this right.

No matter how much practice you do, you'll still be drawn to look at the onscreen image of the interviewer, but at the very least be sure that you look in the lens of your machine:

- When you say hello
- When you are being asked a question
- When you ask a question
- When you are making a critical point
- When you are finishing an answer
- When you make your closing statement about wanting the job
- When you say goodbye

You won't do this successfully without practice, so I do strongly urge doing a few Skype video calls with friends to get a feeling for how you and others typically come across, and to practice looking into the lens rather than at your interviewer's image.

Job Fairs Are for Professionals at All Levels

These events, whether live or virtual, aren't usually seen as being of much value to senior-level professionals, because they are usually supported by companies that are in a significant expansion phase. This typically means large numbers of openings at lower levels. However, a company that is adding significant numbers of employees at less elevated levels is also quite likely to be adding senior people to balance and manage the new teams, even if such senior positions aren't the responsibility of the recruiters representing the company at the job fair.

If you are a more senior professional, in addition to identifying which participating companies are hiring at lower levels in your area of expertise—and thereby getting a good idea of companies that are probably also hiring at higher levels—your goal in attending a job fair (live or virtual) is to discover why and in what areas each participating company is growing.

Having used the job fair for reconnaissance, you can then leverage your networks and the other research tools we've mentioned to identify those names and titles most likely to be involved in the selection cycle, and approach them directly. Mention any intelligence you gathered at the job fair, but not the job fair itself, and say that you know that they are expanding in _____ area. Add that you have long admired the company because of _____, and that you thought this was a good opportunity to find out if the expansion program was also creating openings in *your* area. We'll discuss making marketing presentations in greater depth in the coming chapters.

So far we have looked at how to build the six major social networks, and have reverse-engineered all major job search activities in ways that allow you to leverage your social networks. With the discussion of Skype we move on to *verbal communication*, and in the next chapter we'll discuss how to get the best out of networking conversations.

PART IV

Leveraging Your Social Networks

CHAPTER 16

THE SECRETS OF SUCCESSFUL NETWORKING CONVERSATIONS

In this chapter we will focus on conversations with professional colleagues and how to leverage them to get job leads and other assistance with your job search. Networking conversations are different in focus, structure, and content from the conversations with anyone who has the potential to hire you. In the latter, you will actually be making a marketing presentation, which is a topic we'll address in Chapter 18. For now, we're going to focus on getting the most out of networking conversations.

Your social networks grow in proportion to the energy you put into building them, first in numbers of contacts and then in the way you develop and nurture those contacts. Conversation is the strongest rapport builder, and the number of networking conversations you create—and how intelligently you structure and execute them—has significant impact on the progress of your job search, as well as on the long-term maturity and usefulness of your networks.

Types of Networking Conversations

Networking conversations will be initiated via e-mail and chat, then progress to phone or Skype, and ultimately lead to in-person discussions. All of these communication media are productive, but you develop the best relationships through conversation.

Face time takes much longer, but will usually generate the best results, which is one of the reasons I so strongly recommend membership in professional and alumni associations. Through such organizations your investment in face time is focused on the people most likely to be of help.

However, taking time commitments into consideration, the most productive networking conversations happen over the telephone, so make the effort to keep a sensible balance between time-hungry in-person networking conversations and time-efficient telephone or Skype video conversations. In this chapter we will focus on networking with colleagues and peers over the phone, although the tactics I suggest apply equally well to in-person meetings.

Productive Networking Conversations

Whatever your communication medium, your networking conversation agenda remains the same. The following are ideas for the content and flow of your networking conversations, but obviously you will have to adapt them to the speech patterns that come naturally to you.

Productive networking conversations play out in distinct steps:

Step #1: Introduction

If possible, recall the last memorable interaction the two of you shared; mentioning someone you both know or an industry-related topic can help break the ice. With someone you haven't spoken to before, reviewing their social media profiles can often tell you about common interests, or give you a lead on an interest you don't share but find interesting; this is not a long conversation but merely a friendly opener. Ask what is happening in your contact's personal and professional life; really listen to the reply and respond in a sincere way that shows your engagement. Note and file the personal and professional intelligence you gather.

Step #2: Statement of Your Situation

Prepare a statement that allows you to encapsulate your situation succinctly: "Malcolm, I just got laid off because of the downturn," or "We have a baby on the way, and _____ is a company where there just isn't room for me to grow professionally," or "My job just got sent to Mumbai, so I guess it's time for me to make a move."

Step #3: Information Gathering

When common professional ground exists through an association or other social network, you can assume that your listener will be well disposed toward you. You can repay this goodwill by showing respect for that person's time and politely cutting to the chase: "I have been an accountant with Anderson for the last four years. I work in the small business area, and I'm looking to make a change." Rather than rambling, in fewer than five seconds you have courteously provided a focus. Tell your contacts in general terms what you *do*, not what you *want*—talking about your aspirations reduces your chances of getting leads.

Step #4: Ask for Assistance

Of course, you can immediately launch into asking if your contact has heard about local companies hiring, but you can achieve even more if you are careful to ask your questions in a productive *sequence*.

Great Networking Questions

Here is a sequence of networking questions that will lead you to jobs you would otherwise never hear about. These are the same question sequences asked every day by headhunters the world over, retooled to fulfill your needs.

They follow a logical order, but it might not suit your needs, so as you examine them, figure out what you would ask if you had time for only one question, then if you had time for only two, and so on. The result will be a comfortably prioritized set of questions. Each question you ask should be specific, so avoid time-wasting questions like "How's business these days?" When you're satisfied with your list of questions, put a copy on your computer and/or smartphone, another in your work area at home, and a third in your wallet or purse.

The questions are broken down into categories. For your customized list, you'll want to ask a couple of questions from each of these categories:

Job Lead Questions
Profession-Specific Questions
Leads at Other Companies
Questions for Network Trading
Career Change Versus Job Lead Questions
When You Get a Referral

Job Lead Questions

Do ask:

- "What needs does your company have at present?"
- "Who in the company is most likely to need someone with my background?"
- "Who else in the company might need someone with my background?"
- "Is the company/department planning any expansion or new projects that might create an opening?"
- "When do you anticipate a change in company manpower needs?"
- "Does your company have any other divisions or subsidiaries? Where are they?"
- "I'd appreciate any e-mail addresses or telephone numbers of headhunters you hear from."

Don't ask:

- "Can you or your company hire me?"

Profession-Specific Questions

You might wish to add some profession-specific questions, especially if they can circle back to job leads in some way. For instance, people in Information Technology might ask questions about operating systems, communication or database protocols, or applications and programs used. After receiving an answer, add a similarly focused follow-up question—"Thanks, Gail. Who else do you know that uses these configurations?"—that will lead you to other companies likely to have similar needs. Be sure any question you add to your list is geared toward identifying names, titles, and companies in your areas of interest. When you are given a lead on a company, even if you already know of them, always say thank you and ask a follow-up question: "Thanks Jackie, that's a great lead, I really appreciate it. Do you know anyone I could speak to there?"

When an offer of introduction is made—"Let me speak to Charlene Hogarth for you"—don't rely on your contact to get you into that company. If the door hasn't opened in a few days, it might not. You should execute your own plan of attack, seeking other personal introductions within the company through your networking resources and making direct appeals by telephone, e-mail, and snail mail resume submissions.

Leads at Other Companies

When you are sure that no job openings exist within a particular department or company, move on to gathering leads at other companies. You could ask:

- "Do you know anyone at other banks in town that I could speak with?"

However, you will get a better response if your question is more focused:

- "Who do you know at _____?" or "What's going on at _____?"

Continue this thought by mentioning the names of a few companies you'd like to penetrate. If your contact can't think of anyone, ask about other companies:

- "What companies have you heard about that are hiring now?"
- "If you were going to make a move, which companies would you look at?"
- "Which are the most rapidly growing companies in the area?"

If you are offered two or three company names, remember to backtrack with a request for contact names at each of the companies:

- "Do you know of anyone I could speak to at _____?"

You can also ask for leads at companies you plan to call, or even at those you have already called:

- "Jack, I was planning to contact _____, Inc. Would you happen to know anyone there who could give me a heads-up on what's happening in _____ (department)?"

Questions for Network Trading

When a conversation is going well, and if you are talking to someone in your profession, tack on a last question that gives you job leads to offer people in your social networks:

- "If you don't have a need for someone with my background right now, who are you looking for? Perhaps I might know someone." Or, "What positions is your company trying to fill right now?"

Career Change Versus Job Lead Questions

If you are considering a career change, you might want to research professional life in the field you are contemplating. In this case, after explaining that you are thinking about a particular profession for a new career direction, ask:

- What it is like working in _____ (new profession)
- What your contact likes most and least about the work
- What are the deliverables of your target job
- What are the problems that are central to the job's existence

- What education, experience, and professional behaviors help people succeed in the profession
- Who succeeds and why
- Who fails and why
- How does one move ahead in the profession

The extent of your questioning will depend on the willingness of your contact to continue the conversation; I've known these conversations to run for fifty minutes.

When You Get a Referral

Whenever you are offered a lead, even if it is an obvious one, remember that encouragement is positive reinforcement. When people see that their advice is appreciated, they will often come up with more helpful information.

When you get leads on companies or people to talk to, be sure to thank your networking contact and follow up again with a rapport-building question. Ask to use her name as an introduction. "Thank you, Linda. I didn't know _____ was building a facility in town, and I appreciate getting Holly Barnes's name. May I use your name as an introduction or would you like me to keep it confidential?" The answer will invariably be "yes, you can use my name," but asking demonstrates professionalism and will encourage your contact to come up with more names and leads. "That's very helpful, Bill. Does anyone else come to mind?"

When you get permission to use your contact's name, use it in an introduction: "Holly Barnes? My name is _____. I'm an accounting friend of Bill Smith's. He suggested I call, so before I go any further, Bill asked me to say hello." This is a bridge-building phrase and usually leads to a brief exchange about your mutual contact before you go into your information-gathering agenda. It also quickly forms a common bond.

Although you say thank you at the time of the conversation, it's a nice touch to follow it up with an e-mail (see the latest edition of *Knock 'em Dead Job Search Letter Templates* on the *Knock 'em Dead* website for thank-you letter examples). The positive impression you make might get you another lead, and it never hurts to attach a copy of your resume with the thank-you e-mail.

Wrapping Up a Networking Conversation

When your networking call or face-to-face conversation comes to its natural conclusion, express your willingness to return the favor, and leave the door open for future calls: "Christine, thanks so much for your help. I do appreciate it. At times like this you realize how important your colleagues are, so I'd like to give you my telephone number and e-mail so that one day I might return the favor. Let's stay in touch."

Other statements that you might use at the end of your conversation could include:

- "I'll let you know how it works out with Holly Barnes."
- "Might I get in touch in a couple of months to see if the situation at _____, Inc. has changed?"

You are going to get some pleasant surprises from making networking calls, but also a few disappointments. You will be surprised at how someone you always regarded as a real pal won't give you the time of day while someone you never considered a friend will go above and beyond the call of duty for you. I've come to the conclusion over the years that real friends are not necessarily the people you like the most, but rather the people who see you through the crappy times that come to us all in life.

Networking is a numbers game, so keep initiating conversations with your networking contacts, start every one with an open mind, stay in touch with your contacts regardless of whether they were able to help you, and let them all know when you get a job: "I just landed a job and wanted to say thanks for your help during a difficult time in my life, it meant a lot to me. I hope you never find yourself in that situation, but if you do I'd like to help."

A career lasts a long time, and next week or a decade from now, when a group of managers (including one from your personal network) talk about filling a new position, they will ask, "Who do we know?" That someone is more likely to be you when you are connected in meaningful ways to the members of your online *and* offline networks.

Without conversations taking place, interviews don't get scheduled and job offers don't get made. That's why the focus of a networked job search is always to build and leverage your networks to *get into conversations as quickly and as often as possible with the people who can hire you* and the people who can introduce you to the people who can hire you. You can wait for these conversations to happen, or you can make them happen.

In the next chapter we'll tie together different aspects of the network-integrated job search and learn how to use them to double, triple, and quadruple the number of job interviews you land.

CHAPTER 17

How to Quadruple Your Interviews

Millions of job hunters execute a job search by updating an old resume, responding to job postings, and uploading their ineffective resumes into the job site databases where they sit undiscovered and ignored. Some of them create a half-hearted LinkedIn profile and, believing in the LinkedIn job fairy, sit back and wait for the job offers to pour in.

These millions of job hunters who do nothing to educate themselves about modern job search and career strategy constitute that body of otherwise competent professionals who make up the long-term unemployed. You don't want to become part of this club.

Career professionals estimate that a distinct minority educate themselves in modern career management strategy, invest themselves in creating a resume that will be discoverable in databases, create social media profiles that are similarly visible, and then engage in activities to make themselves even more discoverable by corporate recruiters.

Nevertheless, most of these activities are still essentially passive, because they depend on your being found and approached by recruiters. Job search in these increasingly insecure and competitive times isn't a contemplative sport like fishing. It has much more in common with contact sports like football. In the world of work, if you want something to happen, you have to fight for it.

Multiplying Your Odds of Success

Now it is time to tie all the threads of a network-integrated job search together and lay out a practical strategy for increasing the number of interviews you can generate. The foundation for this, and the overarching goal of your job search every day, is to identify and get into a conversation with anyone who holds any of your identified high-value job titles at any and every company within your target location, using the many proven tactics that we have discussed throughout the book.

The more ways you approach the hiring managers within your target companies (and failing that, the people who know them), the faster and more frequently you will *get into conversations with the people who can and will hire you*. While most job hunters respond to a job lead by uploading a resume into the required database, such an approach gives you only one chance of getting an interview. Although responding to job postings is a big part of most job searches, you can double, triple, and quadruple your chances of getting interviews by making direct approaches to the people in a position to hire you with a sequence of different approaches.

Is the Resume Still Relevant to Job Search?

You might have heard that the resume is outmoded as a job search tool, and that all you need now is a social media profile. However, running your life without a resume is like running an office without paper: It may sound nice, but it isn't going to happen.

The technology advances that birthed the Internet have likewise changed the way companies recruit and working professionals find jobs. Social media sites have given recruiters a truly great resource for finding candidates, and job seekers another great way to make themselves visible. This does not mean the end of the resume, however, because there are distinct differences between these communication tools. As my most esteemed friend and colleague, and America's leading career columnist, Joyce Lain Kennedy says, "Your online profile is not a customized document, but is more like a one-size-fits-all pitch posted on a digital billboard that's located on a busy information superhighway and seen, hopefully, by hordes of unknown viewers."

For recruiters, social media sites essentially constitute another vast resume database that they search with keywords. It's no accident that social media sites want you to upload your resume as part of your profile development, because this is the document recruiters take away with them to show to management. If you have ever spoken to a social media profile writer, you'll also have noticed that the first thing they want from you is your resume as a foundation on which to build the social media profile. A resume remains relevant because it is useful:

- As a passive job search tool. Upload your resume into resume databases, and attach it to your social media profiles, and you increase your visibility to the recruiters who are looking for professionals like you.
- As a template from which you can create different resumes for the different jobs you wish to pursue, and can customize these resumes to the specific needs, priorities, and preferred language of the companies, recruiters, and hiring managers

you wish to approach. You can, and should, always customize your resume to every job and company you approach.

However, we now live in a world where your resume is no longer the only job search document you need; maximum job search effectiveness now demands that your resume and social media profiles work in harmony to hasten the successful conclusion of your transition.

Your resume is the most succinct summary of your career, often forming the foundational document of your social networking profiles, and for recruiters who discover you through resume bank searches and social media database searches, it is the document they pass on to hiring managers. Quite simply, it is the single most valuable financial document you will ever own—ignore it at your peril.

You Have the Foundations for Success

Obviously, if you are on this journey with me, you are paying attention to the changes in job search and career management brought about by improvements in technology. You have built or are building a productive resume and a social networking profile that you can adapt and upload on LinkedIn, Google+, Facebook, Twitter, and perhaps other social networking sites. You've become a reasonably active member of profession-related groups on your social networking platforms, steadily building a network of contacts who also work in your profession and ideally hold one of your target high-value job titles. You have joined professional and alumni associations and become involved with their online and local activities.

When you've seen interesting jobs posted on job sites or through your social networking apps and dashboard, you've uploaded your resume according to the job posting instructions, and where appropriate loaded your resume into resume banks. And you've attended virtual and local job fairs whenever they occur, all the time working back through your social networks to get names and introductions from these activities. Now it is time to weave all the information you've gathered through your networking and other job search activities into an approach that increases the number of job interviews you land.

One Chance to Get an Interview

Whenever you see a posting for a job you can do, respond in the requested way, flagging all contact information for the company: website, mailing address, telephone, and any names and e-mail addresses available from the website.

How to Double Your Interview Odds

E-mail your resume directly to a hiring manager with a personalized cover letter.

This usually presents a big problem: You have many tools and tactics with which to find names that go with high-value job titles, but often you don't have a given manager's e-mail address or any obvious way to get it. Until now.

If you don't have an e-mail address, don't worry; I'm going to share a sequence of tactics that pretty much guarantees you will find it.

First check the company website. Often companies have e-mail addresses for certain staff members listed publicly. This is useful because companies always follow the same format for all employee e-mail addresses, and once you have one, you can be pretty sure that all other e-mail addresses for that company will follow that same format. Additionally:

- You can search your social networking sites using the company name plus target hiring title and check the results for an e-mail address.
- You can search your social networking contacts for people working at the target company.
- You can use the company name as a search term and see whom you are connected to through your *Groups*, *Communities*, conferences, *Circles*, etc., then reach out for a connection.
- Frequently, depending on a variety of factors, the profiles you find will have a visible e-mail address.

Even if you cannot find an example of a company's e-mail address format, there are only six or seven variations in use; for example, it could be:

myate@KnockEmDead.com
m.yate@KnockEmDead.com
m_yate@KnockEmDead.com
MartinYate@KnockEmDead.com
martiny@KnockEmDead.com
Martin@KnockEmDead.com

. . . and perhaps a few others. To prove this to yourself and to establish a comprehensive list of e-mail format variations, check the business-related e-mails you receive over the next few days for their addresses.

Once you have a name and a list of e-mail address variations, you can send your e-mail cover letter pitch with resume attached to each of your e-mail format variations until one goes through rather than bouncing back.

As the primary result, you have established communication with a hiring manager or recruiter as a first step toward *getting into conversation*. The secondary result is that you have side-stepped the problem of your resume languishing in databases or your social media profile getting overlooked. And as if this weren't enough, you now know how to find the e-mail address for anyone else you want to contact at this or any other company.

E-Mail Subject Lines That Get Your E-Mail Read

When sending e-mails—not just job-related e-mails but all e-mails—it is a professional courtesy to provide a revealing and concise subject line that immediately tells the receiver who you are and what you want.

Using a revealing subject line can mean the difference between your e-mail getting opened and getting trashed. The purpose of a good subject line, like a blog headline or tweet, is to grab readers' attention and draw them into the story. With e-mail, a powerful subject line draws readers in, telling them what they are going to be reading about. This means your subject line has to be intriguing and professional. For starters, don't use a subject line that states the obvious, like "Resume" or "Jim Smith's Resume."

If you are responding to a job posting, the job title and job posting number are necessary, but just a start. Combine this factual information with a little intriguing information that reflects the priorities of the job posting. For example:

- Financial Analyst #MB450—CPA/MBA/8 yrs' exp
- Posting 2314—MIT Grad is interested
- Job #6745—Top Sales Professional Here

If you don't have a job posting to give you employer priorities, you can use employer priorities established in your TJD work (see Chapter 5). For example:

- IT Manager—7 yrs. IT Consulting
- Benefits Consultant—Nonprofit Exp in NY
- Referral from Tony Banks—Product Management Job

You can also try subject lines, for example:

- Your next Reg HR Manager—EEOC, FLSA, & ADA

A message in an e-mail inbox will typically reveal a maximum of sixty characters; the above example is just fifty-two characters. An opened e-mail will show a subject line of up to 150 characters that can give a reader further focus and added incentive to read. If you use longer subject lines, make your headline short to ensure visibility in an unopened e-mail. For instance:

- Your next Reg HR Manager—EEOC, FLSA & ADA

Then use the available extra space in an opened e-mail for added detail, for example:

- Your next Reg HR Manager—EEOC, FLSA, ADA, OSHA, T&D. 10 yrs. HR, arbitration, campus, executive recruitment, selection, compensation

If the first forty-one characters help get the e-mail opened, the full subject line can only give the recipient further incentive to read your message. There are other uses for extended subject lines, too. You can use them:

- As Twitter status announcements
- In your discussion group posts that announce your availability

How to Triple Your Interview Odds

Send a resume and personalized cover letter to that manager through *traditional mail*. I know this sounds crazy, but it works. In a digital world, no one gets much traditional mail anymore, which makes receiving it a welcome break from the screen most professionals seem to spend their days staring at, and with this third angle of attack you triple your chances of getting a response and starting a conversation.

I suggest putting your resume in a large flat envelope to stand out, and if you can afford priority mail, you'll guarantee its getting opened almost immediately.

How to Build Communication Bridges in E-Mails and Letters

If you do searches of news media, blogs, and communities, etc. using the names of your target companies, you will frequently find information that you can use as an icebreaker in your e-mails or letters—or conversations for that matter. You can open your e-mail with a mention of the media coverage. This guarantees the rest of your message will be read: Who doesn't like hearing about how wonderful they are? You can also add a link to the information in an e-mail (with a traditional letter, enclose a copy).

It is also very effective when you use the information you've gathered to open a telephone conversation: "I've been meaning to call you ever since I saw the article in . . ."

Multiple E-Mail and Letter Submissions

With larger companies, you may find it worthwhile to make a number of contacts and approaches (as we discussed earlier) to ensure that all the potential players in the recruitment and selection cycle know of your existence.

You won't necessarily send all these communications out at once, but rather spread them over a couple of weeks. Keep a log of your e-mail (and mail) activities so that you can follow up with a phone call.

How to Quadruple Your Interview Odds

Making a follow-up telephone call will quadruple your chances of getting into conversation with a hiring manager. With e-mails, connect within twenty-four to thirty-six hours, and with traditional mail recipients make the follow-up in three to four days. Making calls first thing in the morning, at lunchtime, or at 5 P.M., when gatekeepers are less likely to take your call, will further increase your odds of making the connection; I'd advise excluding Monday morning as everyone is busy getting up to speed for the week. How to deal with gatekeepers is handled in the most recent edition of *Knock 'em Dead: The Ultimate Job Search Guide.*

I Lied about Quadrupling Your Interview Chances—It's More

If you repeat this sequence of approaches with two other high-value management hiring titles, you will have ***twelve times*** better odds of getting a job interview than the person who just responds to a job posting by uploading a resume and patiently waiting for something to happen.

The more frequently you *get into conversations with managers who have the authority to hire you*, the faster you will land that new position, because you have skipped right over the resume database hurdle, sidestepped the recruiters' evaluation process, and made a direct and personal pitch to the actual decision maker.

This is never more important than when the economy is down or in recovery. At such times, your competition is fierce and employers actually do recognize and appreciate the initiative and motivation you display by doing these things, especially picking up the phone and initiating a conversation. We will discuss exactly how to structure these calls and how to handle the flow of question and answer in the next chapter.

CHAPTER 18

INITIATING MARKETING CONVERSATIONS WITH HIRING MANAGERS

You talk to strangers on the phone every day for one reason or another, so don't tell yourself that calling hiring managers is impossible because you feel terrified to pick up the phone and talk to people you don't know. Calling potential employers is on a par with scheduling a dental appointment—you sure as hell don't want to do it, but you do it because it has to be done, and whatever small terrors it causes are far outweighed by what you gain: landing the next step on your career path and a fresh start on managing that career more successfully.

How to Overcome Fear and Loathing

I was an immigrant some thirty-five years ago and I didn't have the luxury of following my passions; I had to eat and pay the bills and I didn't know anyone. My first real job was working as a Silicon Valley headhunter, and this was way before it was a respected professional occupation or the Valley had achieved its world-changing visibility. My employer at the time had a job security program that you won't believe, but

I swear it's true: You made a minimum of seventy-five calls a day and you got to keep your job and come to work tomorrow. I spent every day on the telephone talking to strangers. I had to find companies with job openings, then find someone who could do the job, then put the two together and broker the conversations and the employment agreement. Not a soul knew it at the time, but during every one of the seventy-five to one hundred calls I made every day of every week I was always absolutely terrified. I had nothing and no one to fall back on and so no choice but to learn how to do it.

My terror was part fear and part adrenaline rush, and a big lesson I learned was that the rush we associate with fear is in fact a very natural reaction for anyone engaged in a critical performance activity. I further learned that, like others before me, I could harness that adrenaline jolt and use it to fuel my success.

Four things I learned about harnessing my abject terror might help you:

- Because I was on the phone, no one would know who I was or how scared I felt and looked.
- I knew that I would never meet these people unless they were interested in what I had to offer, in which case they'd be happy I called.
- Rejection of my offered services was not rejection of me as a person.
- Sales is a numbers game and every "no" simply brought me closer to the next "yes."

My next discovery was that professionals are trained to be respectful of others and that most people I talked to were pleasant and friendly in that uniquely American way. It gradually dawned on me that there was a precise blueprint for how to make almost every call successful in some way. As a result, I became successful, and over the years climbed to a position of global recognition and respect for training other headhunters in how to make every call successful by using multitasking—a brand new phrase back then.

If a deeply orthodox coward like me can make profitable calls to strangers, you have to believe there's a workable methodology behind it. There is, and it all starts with having clear goals for what you want a call to achieve with each one you make.

Multiple Goals Multiply Odds of Success

If you have just one goal when you pick up the phone—to get an interview—you have just one chance of success but many more for failure, and that increases the pressure. When headhunters make sales/marketing calls, they have multiple goals in mind, and I have adapted these goals to fit your needs in executing a successful job search PDQ. Every marketing call you make should have these goals:

1. I will arrange an interview.
2. If my contact has no openings, I will find out when she will have openings.
3. I will develop leads on job openings elsewhere in this company.
4. I will develop leads on job openings in other companies.
5. I will get names to talk to for each of these other jobs.
6. I will leave the door open to talk with this person again in the future.
7. If my contact is busy, I will arrange another time to talk.

Adopt these goals for your marketing calls, and any conversation you have with anyone during your job search, because every conversation holds the potential to turn into an interview or lead you toward another conversation that will generate first a phone conversation and then a face-to-face meeting.

As I said a few paragraphs back: If you have just one goal with a call, you have just one chance of success but many more for failure, and that increases the pressure. But if you have multiple goals for your call, you have multiple chances for success and you minimize the chances of doom and gloom that come with a failed call.

Why Smart Managers Like Your Calls

You might worry about calling people directly because you are concerned that they will be annoyed by the perceived intrusion. This is a misconception: The first responsibility of every manager is to get work done through others, so any intelligent executive is always on the lookout for talent, if not for today, then for tomorrow. If that isn't enough to allay your fears, keep in mind that the person on the other end of the line has very possibly been in your position and is sensitive to your situation. As long as you cut to the chase, and are concise and professional, you'll find that the majority of people you contact will be respectful and helpful whenever they can.

Paint a Word Picture

The secret to painting a word picture that gets results is being succinct. Your goal is to build an initial introduction and presentation that comes in at well under a minute. If you do this, your call won't be considered an intrusion.

Within that initial presentation, you need to paint a comprehensive picture of your most critical skills, keeping it brief out of courtesy, and avoid giving too much information that could rule you out of consideration. You can do this by referring back to your TJD and the social media profiles you created with it, but an even more effective approach is to refer to the concise six-line Performance Summary you created from your TJD work and used on your resume and social media profiles.

How to Organize and Sequence Marketing Conversations

Writing notes for something you're going to say aloud is very different from writing something to be read. If you write out full sentences and then try to read them aloud to someone over the phone, you'll sound like those stuttering telemarketers who call every night to read you their script just as you're sitting down to dinner (be thankful you don't have *that* job).

Speech is more casually structured than the written word, and you'll get the best results if you write down the bullet points you want to make in your presentation rather than full sentences, so that you can't read it word for word. Once you have written it out, speak it aloud a few times until you have the flow, then reduce the word count until each bullet point can fit on a single line. Practice it with a friend or record yourself for critique until you are comfortable with the content and the rhythm; you'll also learn how long your presentation will run. Keep it under one minute. You don't have to share all your skills, just enough to arouse the listener's interest and get a conversation going.

Step #1

Give the hiring manager or recruiter a snapshot of who you are and what you do. You want to give her a reason to stay on the phone. If you have an introduction from a networking colleague, build a bridge with that:

"Miss Shepburn? Good morning, my name is Martin Yate, and our mutual friend Greg Spencer suggested I call . . ." There will then follow a brief exchange about your mutual colleague and you'll feel the barriers come down a little.

Alternatively, you may have gotten the name and contact information from, for example, a professional association database, in which case you will use that as a bridge:

"Miss Shepburn? My name is Martin Yate. We haven't spoken before, but as we are both members of the _____ Association, I hoped you could spare me a couple of minutes to give me some advice . . ."

When she agrees, you can go into the rest of your presentation. If at any point your contact says or implies by tone that she is busy, ask when would be a good time to reconnect.

When you prioritized employer needs in the TJD exercise, you used your list to build the Summary for your social media profiles, and if you were writing a resume, you condensed them into three to six short sentences for your Performance Summary. From your TJD work, you already know what aspects of your experience have the widest and most relevant appeal, and all you have to do is translate them into the bullet points that encourage a smooth verbal presentation:

"Miss Shepburn? My name is Martin Yate. We haven't spoken before, but as we are both members of the _____ Association, I hoped I might get a couple of minutes of your time for some advice . . ."

You pause for agreement, then start with the opening line from your resume's Performance Profile or social media bio, for example:

"I'm a senior technology sales associate with a track record in B-to-B office technology sales, selling to corporations, institutions, and small businesses."

You might take out some information—for example, describing yourself as experienced, rather than identifying a specific number of years in your field. This encourages the listener to qualify your statement with a question: "How much experience do you have?" Any question denotes a level of interest and might well mean that a job exists.

Step #2

Step 2 introduces your *professional brand* with a statement about what you have achieved and what you can deliver:

"As the number three salesperson in my company, I increased sales in my territory 15 percent, to over one million dollars. In the last six months, I won three major accounts from my competitors—a hospital, a bank, and a technology start-up."

Note that you always talk about *what* you can do, but never *how* you do it, because this approach encourages questions—and questions show interest.

Step #3

Get to the reason for your call and get the conversation started:

"The reason I'm calling is that I'm looking for a new challenge, and I felt we might have some areas of common interest. Are these the types of skills and accomplishments you look for in your sales associates?"

Notice that your presentation doesn't end with a needy "Have you got a job? Can you hire me?" Rather it closes with a question that encourages a positive response and opens the possibility of conversation.

After your question, you can expect a short silence on the other end of the line. Be patient, as the employer may need a few seconds to digest your words. The response will either be a question, denoting interest, or it will be an objection. Whichever response you get, give short, reasonable answers, and when it makes sense to do so, finish your reply with a question. Just as an employer's questions show interest in you, your questions should show interest in the work you could do in that department.

Here's an example of how such a conversation might proceed. Because you and I come from different backgrounds, we will never speak alike, so with the following sample questions and answers just capture the essence and tailor it to your own speech patterns.

"... *The reason I'm calling is that I'm looking for a new challenge, and as I know and respect your product line, I felt we might have areas for discussion. Are these the types of skills and accomplishments you look for in your staff?*"

[Pause.]

Miss Shepburn: "*Yes, they are. What type of equipment have you been selling?*" [Buy signal.]

You: "*A comprehensive range from work stations to tablets, through routers and modems to printers and ink . . . and all the peripherals you would expect. I sell to my customers' needs and the capabilities of the technology. I have been noticing a considerable interest in _____ recently. Has that been your experience?*"

Miss Shepburn: "*Yes, I have actually.*" [Useful information for you.] "*Do you have a degree?*" [Buy signal.]

You: "*I come from circumstances that required me to start work early, but I'm doing courses at night for a BS in Communications.*"

Miss Shepburn: "*Our customer base is very sophisticated, and they expect a certain professionalism and competence from us.*" [An inkling of the kind of person the company wants to hire.] "*How much experience do you have?*" [Buy signal.]

You: "*Well, I've worked in both operations and sales, so I understand sales and the fulfillment process. My customers benefit from not having to deal with false expectations, because I understand how to work cooperatively with fulfillment.*" [General but thorough.] "*How many years of experience are you looking for?"* [Turning it around, but furthering the conversation.]

Miss Shepburn: *"Ideally, four or five for the position I have in mind."* [More good information.] *"How many do you have?"* [Buy signal.]

You: *"I have over four and a half, so it sounds like I could fit right in with your needs."*

Miss Shepburn: *"What's your territory?"* [Buy signal.]

You: *"I cover the metropolitan area. Miss Shepburn, it sounds as if we might have something to talk about. I could come in Monday or Tuesday of next week; would either of those days work for you?"* [Encourage Miss Shepburn to decide *which* day she can see you, rather than *whether* she will see you.]

Your questions show interest, carry the conversation forward, and teach you more about the company's needs. When you turn a one-sided examination of skills into a two-way conversation between two professionals with a common interest, you dramatically distance yourself from the competition. By the end of the conversation you could have an interview arranged. You can learn how to deal with specific questions in *Knock 'em Dead Job Interview.*

How to Deal with Objections

By no means will every presentation call you make be met with a few simple questions and then an invitation to interview. Sometimes the silence will be broken with an objection. This usually comes in the form of a statement, not a question. The full range of objections you could face are handled in *Knock 'em Dead Job Interview*, and we have limited space here, so we'll just address the two most common objections:

1. "You'll have to talk to Human Resources."
2. "I don't need anyone like you right now."

These might seem like brush-off lines, but they can be turned into interviews, and when that isn't possible, they can almost always generate job leads elsewhere.

In dealing with objections, nothing is gained by confrontation, while much can be gained by an appreciation of the other's viewpoint. Consequently, most objections you hear are best handled by first demonstrating that you see things through the other person's eyes. Start your responses with phrases like "I understand," or, "I can appreciate your position," or, "I see your point," or, "Of course." Follow up with statements like "However," or, "Also consider," or a similar line that allows the opportunity for rebuttal and to gather more information. Again, you can learn specific responses to more than 100 tough questions and objections in *Knock 'em Dead Job Interview.*

"You'll Have to Talk to Human Resources."

When you are told this, ask whom you should speak to in HR and what specific position you should mention. You cover a good deal of ground with this response: You either establish a job title and the fact that an opening exists, or you discover that there is no opening and you are being fobbed off on HR. If there is a job, develop a specific job-related question to ask while the employer is answering the first question: If you can steer the conversation toward the nuts and bolts of the job, and show yourself as someone who understands the issues, your conversation might take a turn. If not, at least you will know more about the job, and will be prepared to have a more informed conversation with the recruiter in HR.

Then, armed with your newly acquired insights, you can talk to HR about your conversation: *"I've just been talking to Jim*

Grant about the Accounts Receivable position, the one where they are having the issues with cash flow. I'm an A/R accountant who has reduced 30-day+ payables by up to 30 percent in my last job, and Jim thought we should talk."

If there is an opening for someone with your talents, your Q&A with the hiring manager (or other contact) will pay off and you will be taken seriously.

If not, don't look at HR as a roadblock; depending on your title and area of expertise, there could be a number of different departments that could use your talents. HR is probably the only department that knows all the openings. In fact, with larger companies, HR can help you arrange interviews in more departments and for different jobs.

"I Don't Need Anyone Like You Right Now."

By no means will every hiring manager you call have a job opening that fits your skills, but you can still turn calls that don't result in interviews into successes. So let's turn now to getting live leads from dead ends.

Live Leads from Dead Ends

We established that your networking and marketing presentation calls should have multiple goals: to arrange an interview, arrange another time for a conversation, send a resume for future follow-up if you haven't done so already, and develop leads on job openings with this company in the future and with other companies for now. With the right questions, your contact could well give you an introduction to someone who needs someone exactly like you.

There are five categories of questions that can lead you to job openings and interviews:

1. Leads on other jobs in the department
2. Leads on other jobs in the company
3. Leads on other jobs in other divisions of the company
4. Leads on other jobs in other companies
5. Contacts in other companies

So if there isn't a need for someone like you right now, you can ask:

- *"When do you anticipate new needs in your area?"*
- *"May I send you my resume and keep in touch for when the situation changes?"*
- *"Who else in the company might have a need for someone with my background and skills?"*
- *"What other companies might have a need for someone with my background?"*

If the response is positive:

- *"Thanks, that's a great idea. Whom should I speak to at _____ (company)?"*
  If the response to *that* is positive:

- *"May I mention your name?"*
  Mention a company you plan to call:

- *"Do you know anyone I could speak to at _____?"*
  If you ask just this sequence of questions, you will get leads and introductions, and the last question enables you to open that next call with:
  "Hello, Mr. Jones? My name is Martin Yate, Chuck Harris gave me your name and said to tell you hello . . ."

By asking your personalized versions of these questions, you will achieve some measure of success from every call, leaving you energized and with a feeling of achievement after each conversation. This approach worked for me, and it works for every headhunter in the world every day, so it will probably work for you.

Marketing Calls Are Networking Calls

Marketing calls and networking calls are very similar, inasmuch as they follow a similar flow. The following schematic reflects the flow of the above sequence of questions: Get an interview; if not, get a lead on an interview elsewhere.

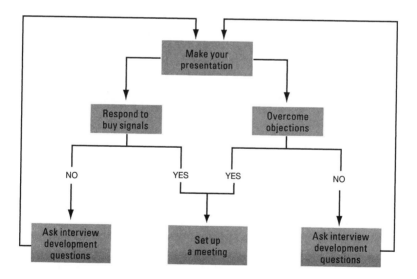

Because networking and marketing calls are continuous activities when you are in transition, it might be a useful reminder to print this out and put it in your work area, where it can be a constant reminder to you during marketing and networking calls.

You Can Do It

Yes, you will probably trip over your tongue a few times when you first start making networking and marketing presentation calls, but you have made similar calls in the course of both your professional and personal life. The key factor in your favor is that everyone you call will be sympathetic, because they have either been in your situation or worry about it happening in the future. After the first ten or so calls you'll find that reaching out and *getting into conversation with people who hold the authority to hire you* is really much easier and more straightforward than you imagined; and with a sequence of planned networking questions to ask, you can make almost every marketing call a success.

CHAPTER 19

SOCIAL NETWORKING AND
ALL YOUR TOMORROWS

Career Management Theory Is Broken

The traditional career management theory of "Choose a profession, get a job, work hard, and be loyal above all things" is broken. That mantra of "hang in no matter what happens and you will be rewarded with long-term employment and financial security" is a myth. Corporations cannot and do not care about your well-being; they only care about your productivity now.

So when you look forward into a world of work where the only constant is change, realize that the most important professional skills you can possess are the skills that ensure your employability and economic stability. Any viable career management strategy for the future must focus on economic viability rather than blind loyalty to a corporate employer.

Social Networks Establish Professional Connectivity

Life is a marathon, not a sprint, and to survive and prosper you need to put your job search today into the context of what will probably be a fifty-year work life. This work life will present you with twists and turns that you could never imagine, and the only way to win is by getting more serious about guiding the trajectory of your professional life. This requires that you stay current with the issues facing your industry and understand how they will impact your job today, and your professional future tomorrow.

The best way to achieve this critical understanding of what is happening in your professional world is to get connected to the committed professionals who make up the majority of social networks, and who along with you make up the inner circle of your profession. These most committed professionals, naturally leveraging the power of crowdsourcing in their networking activities, are invariably the best informed about coming changes, which skills will dominate, who will keep their jobs and prosper, and who will wash out. You discover these insights through the collective wisdom of your social networks: LinkedIn, Google+, Facebook, Twitter, plus alumni and professional associations. Collectively, these networking activities will help you connect with like-minded professionals who are as serious about their professional viability as you are.

Sharing ongoing community ties with these peers will increase both your professional credibility and visibility, and will alert you to the cutting-edge technologies that are about to revolutionize your profession yet again. The enhanced professional insight that results from interaction with your networks will also alert you if your company or even your entire profession is about to experience the kind of seismic change that could cost you your job. Advance notice of the coming storm can be a lifesaver.

The Tools for Navigating a Long Career

Statistically, your jobs will last an average of about four years, which means that you will probably experience twelve to fifteen job changes over the course of your entire professional career. Some changes will be your choice, while others may well be forced on you. To survive and prosper over the stretch of a long career that might include this many job changes, some of them entirely unexpected, you need to develop new career management skills that no one ever told you were important. In fact, these skills are so important that they have been downplayed, because they give you more control of your life, and the corporation less.

Essential Skills for Career Success

The tools you absolutely need to master for your long-term financial stability in a professional world that offers a complete lack of stability are:

1. How to put a resume together
2. How to build social networks
3. How to integrate your networks into a job search strategy that generates job interviews
4. How to turn those interviews into job offers

This last is almost certainly your weakest professional skill, because you have had limited education in, or real world practice at, making job offers happen.

Once you land that next job it is a new day, and an opportunity to close your eyes and dream that all is now secure again—until the next recession and next job search. Because the latest labor-saving technology is always implemented during economic downturns, you will notice that many of those jobs aren't coming back.

Alternatively, you could become better informed and more realistic about life in a corporate career, and take a more careful look at strategies that give you more control, like how to:

1. Start that new job on the right foot.
2. Make that job more secure.
3. Continue development of the *transferable skills and professional values* that are the foundation of success in every profession.
4. Win access to the inner circles that exist within every department, because this is where the plum assignments, special training, raises, and promotions live.
5. Plan and execute confidential job searches and career changes while you are employed.
6. Build and nurture networks to ease transitions.

Why are these skills so important? Because they are the skills that keep a roof over your head and put food on your table; they are the skills that give you more control over the path your career takes. They are the skills that empower you to get more of what you want out of life.

Keeping Your Brand on Track

Integral to this new approach to career management is the creation and maintenance of a resilient *professional brand* and the ability to keep it visible within your social networks. You are probably only starting to do this now because you are engaged in a job search. But your evolving *professional brand* and the health of your networks going forward will come into play every time you experience both planned and unplanned transitions. The intelligence you gather through your social networking activities will greatly diminish those unplanned transitions. In short, your establishment and maintenance of a desirable professional presence on your professional networks will play an ever-increasing role in helping you maintain economic stability, live a meaningful life, and achieve enduring success.

Become a Source of Knowledge to Your Networks

Most people let their social networks die once they are settled in a new job, believing with all the innocence of Peter Pan that all is now well again, now and forever, amen. In doing so, they let their brand and visibility die along with their networks. It is a challenge to manage growing networks, but we all have to adapt to the realities of modern life and, recognizing its insecurities, make social networking part of our own private social safety net.

One of the answers to this challenge is maintaining a networking presence without having it become a chore and take over your life. To help you do this there are technology tools like Google Alerts and the other information-gathering apps and dashboard tools that help you gather profession-relevant intelligence for your networking activities. Curate and share the best results these resources deliver with your networks and you will stay current with the news and changes that affect your professional world with minimal encroachment on your time.

Once you have professionally interesting content to share, you need only a couple of sentences to introduce it, and can then use tools like Hootsuite to spread it around your social networks. Your networks will see you as a *team player* and a source of useful information. You will stay visible on countless radars and you will be better informed about the strategies and tactics that will help you maintain your career.

Stay Visible to High-Value Networks

You might also use such news items in personal e-mails. All you need is one form letter that can be personalized to each recipient, and a link to the article. These e-mails go to your immediate circle of colleagues and that special group of the high-value contacts you discovered on each of your social media platforms during your job search. Because the high-value contacts who hold those job titles one, two, and three or more title levels above you will still be higher up the ladder when next you plan a strategic move, it's smart to maintain a degree of visibility and credibility in the eyes of people who can have such influence over your professional future.

It's Your Life

You can say I'm a cynic, but I have watched the world of employment for my entire adult life and I know only too well how employers treat employees at all levels: They will suck you dry and spit you out just as soon as they can find someone cheaper, export your job to Mumbai, or automate it out of existence. "It's nothing personal," they tell you; "It's just business." You need a strategy that counterbalances these despicable realities, a plan that gives you more control of your destiny.

Networks: Your Best Lifeline

The people involved in social networks are active because they realize that they need the help of their professional peers and colleagues—they need the help of human beings to weather the storms of a long career. Having well-built and conscientiously maintained networks will give you the inside contacts, collective wisdom, and emotional support to help you navigate the many twists and turns you'll experience through a half-century work life. You will earn that support with the help you offer others in their times of need.

You and MeInc

When a company dispenses with your services, it's nothing personal: The company is doing what it must do to survive and satisfy the shareholders. You need to do the same thing: Take control of your life, your economic survival, and your success by taking more responsibility for what happens in your life. Start thinking of yourself as a company—as MeInc, a financial entity that must survive and prosper over half a century.

Such enlightened self-interest means placing *your* financial survival and personal fulfillment front and center in your life. I want you to stop thinking of yourself as some poor sap looking for a job, and think of yourself instead as a company, a financial entity that must maintain a steady cash flow over the long haul.

What Do You Want Your Life to Become?

All career management decisions should be made while keeping in mind long-term goals like "What do I want my life to become?" Give thought to your endgame: where you want to be and what you want your life to be like five, ten, and twenty years from now. Then work backward from there to the present. When you know clearly where you stand today and have clearly defined goals for the future, you have steppingstones to take you step by step toward achievement of your goals.

Steppingstones to Freedom and Security

Why not invest your time and energy in making your life unfold in ways that are meaningful to you? Take your dreams and turn them into concrete goals by identifying the stepping-stones that will bring them to life. Then take those stepping-stones and in the spaces between each one identify the smaller steps you'll need to take to carry you forward to the next major steppingstone along your path.

Then break each of those steps down into ever-smaller actions, until there is always some tiny step you can take tonight after work, some minor action that you can take on the weekend, that will bring you inexorably toward your life goals. Each small step you take gives you a more meaningful life and brings you closer to making your dreams a reality.

Live Up to Your Dreams

Like life, a successful career is a marathon, not a sprint; whatever your goals, the sooner you start toward them the better. Begin studying for that degree or that real estate license, take that painting class, or read that book on what makes entrepreneurs tick. Watch and learn how companies succeed and why they fail. Do it, because you *can* do it, and you have the right to do it, for yourself and for a more secure future.

This constant din of consumerism pulls your attention away from working toward a meaningful life for yourself. It encourages you to indulge in fantasies, living up to your income rather than living up your dreams. The result, all too often, is that you get in over your head, and, trapped like a mouse on a paddle wheel, you are too busy running in place to ever think about how you can make the dreams of your life come true by steadily pursuing parallel *entrepreneurial* and *dream career* alternatives. (For more on this, see *Knock 'em Dead: Secrets & Strategies for Success in an Uncertain World*.)

Live Life Like You Mean It

Don't think you have made it because you believe some employer owes you for all the hard work, sacrifice, and loyalty.

Don't deceive yourself; get involved in the scrimmage of life and make it work on your terms. Stop watching your life whiz by on the screen, stop training to be a good consumer and an obedient drone. Instead, invest your personal time in you—*in what you want from this wonderful thing called life*—and take full advantage of being alive at the beginning of this wonderful digital era, with all its tools and opportunities just waiting for you to use them and make your dreams a reality.

Social Networking Increases Your Odds for a Successful Life

Corporations have no intent but to squeeze you dry and throw you on the trash heap. And while you cannot change this uncontestable horror, you can mitigate its impact on your life. While corporations won't help you, people will, especially the people who know you: the peers and colleagues who make up your networks. In a world without professional security, the creation of networks full of people relevant to your career objectives is your most valuable resource for economic viability, career success, and a life lived on your terms.

INDEX